Who Has Y

Who Has Your Back? is an essential read for modern-day leaders. Laurie Arron brilliantly captures the essence of support for effective leadership and the pivotal role of the Chief of Staff. Drawing on real-world examples and keen observations, this book offers invaluable insights that resonate with my own experiences in leadership coaching. Any leader looking to maximize their support system and thrive in today's fast-paced environment should keep this guide close at hand.

> —DR. MARSHALL GOLDSMITH is the Thinkers50 #1 Executive Coach and *New York Times* bestselling author of *The Earned Life*, *Triggers*, and *What Got You Here Won't Get You There*

This book is a must-read for every overwhelmed, exhausted, and frustrated CEO. I've coached founders of multimillion-dollar companies, presidents of banks, and senior executives in Hollywood. They all carry a large burden. If you ask them, "Who's got your back?" they laugh—or even worse, they sigh deeply. For a CEO who craves more time and more freedom, the ultimate leverage is a new hire. A Chief of Staff will help you have more energy and inner peace than you ever thought possible. This book is your guide. And it's designed to be read on a short flight. Get your copy now. You can thank me later.

> —RICH LITVIN, high-performance coach and bestselling author of *The Prosperous Coach*

Laurie's book brilliantly illuminates how a skilled Chief of Staff can transform chaos into order, ideas into action, and vision into reality. A must-read for CEOs, Chiefs of Staff, or anyone aspiring to navigate the complex landscapes of business successfully.

> —RALPH DE LA VEGA, former Vice Chairman, AT&T Inc., and author of *Obstacles Welcome*

Thanks to Laurie's expertise in optimizing the CEO–Chief of Staff relationship, we drove high impact throughout our organization. Her book crystallizes the vital leadership strategies that have strengthened relationships and alignment throughout our team and amplified our performance. A must-read for leaders aiming for the win, both on and off the court.

—**R. C. BUFORD,** CEO, Spurs Sports & Entertainment

In my role as Chief of Staff, driving collaboration and alignment with our CEO and leadership team is critical. Laurie's book offers insights and a framework that have informed many of our operations, and we will continue to reference these valuable lessons as we move forward.

—**ALISON NABATOFF,** Chief of Staff, Spurs Sports & Entertainment

Practical and inspirational. Fostering a successful team dynamic starts with promoting disruptive thinking and empowering your Chief of Staff to unlock a culture of ideas and innovation for the broader team—and this book taps into that collective potential.

—**THADDEUS ARROYO,** Chief Strategy
and Development Officer, AT&T

In the high-stakes game of corporate growth, the CEO–Chief of Staff bond is your secret weapon. Laurie offers a blueprint for unlocking its power. As COO at Spanx, I can vouch for this dynamic's transformative impact. Laurie's book is essential for CEOs looking to elevate their leadership.

—**DAVID WASILEWSKI,** former COO and CFO, SPANX

An impactful playbook for leaders who want to maximize performance and build a winning culture through a trusted partnership with their Chief of Staff.

—**RASESH PATEL,** President, Vivint

Transformative and thought-provoking. Laurie provides actionable guidance on how to find the right Chief of Staff and set them up for success!

—GLENN LURIE, former President & CEO of AT&T Mobility and Consumer Operations, venture capitalist, board member

Laurie's years of experience as a Chief and consultant come to life through her new book. As a CEO, I am always looking for guidance in an easy-to-digest form. Laurie's book provides a comprehensive yet digestible roadmap regarding how to find, hire, and launch a Chief. This is a must-read for anyone who has a Chief or is contemplating securing a Chief. And new Chiefs will be favorably impacted by the read as well.

—TINO MANTELLA, CEO, Turknett Leadership Group

Having had the privilege to work alongside Laurie in her role as Chief of Staff, I am thrilled to endorse this innovative book. Her book provides exceptional insights into the dynamics between a CEO and their Chief of Staff. If you're a leader looking to optimize your organization's performance, consider this book your new playbook.

—RICK WELDAY, Executive Vice President and General Manager, AT&T Enterprise Markets

Want to scale your impact in an era of increasing demands on your time? This book gives you the strategic blueprint for doing so through finding, hiring, and working with your ideal Chief of Staff. Not only does the author demystify how to work with a Chief of Staff, but you'll also feel that Laurie Arron is genuinely in your corner.

—SANYIN SIANG, CEO Advisor and Duke University Professor

Far more than a guide—Laurie's book is the "Good to Great" for that dynamic relationship between CEOs and Chief of Staff, as well as the overall arc of leadership in the workplace. It is a staple on my shelf of best business books.

—**CLIFF OXFORD,** Founder, CliffCo
and Oxford Center for Entrepreneurs
and author of *Know Grow Exit*

Coupling my experience as a healthcare CEO and former Chief of Staff, I can attest that Laurie's book is a vital blueprint for optimizing leadership and achieving organizational goals. A must-read for anyone in an executive role.

—**MICHAEL YOUNT,** CEO, Avita Pharmacy

WHO HAS YOUR BACK?

A LEADER'S GUIDE TO GETTING THE SUPPORT YOU NEED

from the

CHIEF OF STAFF

YOU DESERVE

LAURIE ARRON

modern wisdom
PRESS

Modern Wisdom Press
Boulder, Colorado, USA

www.modernwisdompress.com

Cover design by Melinda Martin

Author photo courtesy of Romy Modlin

ISBN: 978-1-951692-34-6 (paperback), 978-1-951692-35-3 (epub)

DISCLAIMER

Contents

Foreword

Senior business leaders often find themselves with more projects and ideas than they can personally manage. The most effective leaders find a way to filter these projects into two categories: tasks that require personal attention and those better suited for delegation. These same successful leaders often discover that the best way to achieve this corporate triage is by partnering with a great Chief of Staff.

Through her savvy and straightforward prose, author Laurie Arron shares her expertise and teaches us how to find and hire an outstanding Chief of Staff, and then partner with them to realize results. Senior leaders ready to improve their productivity will find this book a powerful arsenal for achieving their goals.

I crossed paths with Laurie about 20 years ago, when I led AT&T's global connectivity business. Even as a young employee, Laurie was somewhat legendary within the company. She quickly climbed the ranks from a basic, fully commissioned sales representative—where she consistently ranked first or second in wireless sales for the company—to a senior leadership role managing significant corporate clients.

Once, we were about to head into a meeting with a major player in the global transportation business who had questions and concerns about the new international capabilities of mobile phones and devices. Laurie invited me to the meeting to lend expertise in my domain. Strong preparation is one of Laurie's superpowers—then and now. The meeting began with three of us presenting to 20 skeptical business leaders in this global organization. Questions and concerned statements interrupted the presentation immediately. And like a gold medal Olympic fencer, Laurie parried each question with an empathetic, intelligent response. "Oh, that won't do." "We have to change this." "I see why you are so concerned." "We can address that." I hardly said anything, but fifteen minutes in, the meeting had transformed from a tension-filled room to a collaborative problem-solving session. Three months later, the company placed its largest order ever, and it remains a loyal client to this day.

Laurie continued to produce resolutions like this one as her career blossomed at AT&T. She excelled in regional, national, and multinational corporate sales, and held roles in customer experience and community development in AT&T's top-tier markets. She transitioned quickly through these roles, with each advancement producing more success than the one before. Leveraging this diversified experience, Laurie took her hands-on knowledge into the realm of Chiefs of Staff, and in my opinion, she became one of the most distinguished Chiefs of Staff at AT&T, serving several of our senior officers in that capacity.

Laurie's three greatest attributes as a Chief of Staff were her unwavering loyalty, organizational skills, and knack for prioritization (helping her executives focus on the most critical, company-affecting tasks). Laurie has a unique ability to convey hard truths, deliver tough news, provide constructive feedback, and make difficult suggestions with a kind, firm hand. She once "reminded" me that I might want to consider listening more and talking less, a lesson I have not forgotten. (She wasn't even my Chief of Staff, just a concerned colleague.)

Many leaders find that their Chiefs of Staff could be more effective. Too often, the role slips into that of a glorified Executive Assistant, providing excellent administrative work but falling far short of the potential for partnership inherent in such positions. Laurie's smart, practical, and informative book will guide you in finding and hiring the right Chief of Staff. It also provides strategies for enriching relationships with your existing Chief of Staff, if you have one already. Her intriguing client stories align with sound advice and practical concepts to make solutions appear easily and readily applicable. This book is a quick and enjoyable read, as well as a comprehensive guide that will equip you with everything you need to know to find and develop a stellar Chief of Staff.

Regain control of your time and discover the secrets to your next level of success. Laurie Arron has the firsthand knowledge to guide you in finding out what makes a successful Chief of Staff and nurturing your perfect match.

—WILLIAM HAGUE,
former CEO of Tillman Infrastructure
and former EVP International, AT&T

A Takeoff-to-Landing Read That Could Change Your Life

"I want to put a ding in the universe."

— STEVE JOBS

I can't put a ding in the universe. But if you're a C-suite leader, I can put one in your life. And the one I'm offering you is called a Chief of Staff.

Start this book on the runway at JFK, and before you touch down at Chicago O'Hare, you'll have all the knowledge you need to revolutionize your life as a leader. This isn't a long or heavy read. It's written to support, not suffocate. And I don't want to waste your time. Or mine! In my experience, there's no problem that can't be solved in 30 minutes.

If You Only Have a Few Minutes, Here's the Gist:

You will drive the highest impact as a leader when you have the time and energy to focus on what you've committed to doing.

But that's impossible when you are pulled in a thousand directions, trying to resolve every issue and attend every meeting.

You need a strategic partner whose first responsibility is to YOU. To clear your path. To remove distractions. To iron out problems before they reach you. To transform your life. To have your back.

> **You need a strategic partner whose first responsibility is to YOU.**

Your Chief of Staff will be your ally. Your strategic partner. The soul of your team. The catalyst who can ignite your inner fire, allowing you to focus on your top priorities. In this book, you'll get the whys and the hows of engaging this pivotal player.

Why Listen to Me?

There are a lot of books about business out there. You've probably read your share. This one's different. It's not the result of a PhD or a huge research project. I'm not an academic or theoretician. I've led in the heart of corporate culture for decades. I've operated with an observant eye. I've been a Chief of Staff to C-suite leaders. Now I advise them both. I know what you need because I've provided it and I've seen what happens when it's absent.

I spent 30+ years at a Fortune 10 company, initially in entry-level sales. I started off cold calling to sell wireless car phones. This was way back in the days of the brick phone before our pocket technology got smart. I worked hard to identify prospects. I persisted. I would do what it took to close the deal. When my coworkers were taking a lunch break, I was jumping into the trunks of cars to properly fit the technology. I could clinch a sale by the time they settled the check. Little did I know that I was already training to become a Chief of Staff.

Back then, I loved the thrill of a win. The satisfaction of a close. I won my share of sales prizes, from cruises to cash to holidays abroad. In short, I delivered. I held fourteen unique roles and earned nine promotions during my time in corporate. I ran regional and national sales teams supporting multinationals from HP to IBM and GE. It was one hell of an education. I managed and led others, thriving on igniting their fire. I have always had an insatiable hunger and will to succeed. It didn't hurt that I've also always had huge helpings of common sense. I learned to serve and lead the hard way, *and* I loved every minute of it.

Managing multimillion-dollar revenue streams meant I was on first-name terms with the C-suite on a regular basis. Over my career, I experienced seven company acquisitions and five full-on integrations at the closest quarters. I succeeded, I failed, I grew through overwhelming challenges. I learned so much in the throes of these experiences.

I've lived in six cities. Each made its mark on me. I arrived in New York single and polite. I left with a husband, two kids, and a sackful of experience and skills. Working through the years with amazing people and leaders who invested in me and believed in me, I developed a powerful mindset, and I knew how to get sh*t done.

Promotion to Chief

Those stories of my past only matter because they led me to my favorite and most rewarding role: Chief of Staff. The first time I held this role, I served one of our CEOs, who ran a $72B revenue stream at that time. When he retired, I then Chiefed for his two successors. All at one of the biggest companies on Earth, AT&T. My mission was to serve through hard work, candor, and a relentless appetite for delivering strong results.

"Chiefing" changed everything for me. The way I viewed relationships. The way I viewed productivity. And the way I viewed the dynamics of business. The key for me when I served as a Chief of Staff was to look out for my Chief executive and his mission. To prevent problems. To clear the way so he could drive the biggest impact possible.

Years ago, I managed one of AT&T's top accounts, the world's biggest global transportation company. As you might imagine, their brand was reliant on our company's network. Our technology kept them moving. If there was ever an issue with coverage or a dropped call, guess who was first on the phone to explain it to the shipping company's C-suite team?

I loved it. And here's a spoiler: Never recruit a Chief of Staff who would shy from that kind of conversation. Some might "coincidentally" find an important meeting or a dental appointment they couldn't duck. Not me. I welcomed the challenging conversation coming my way. I wanted to be in the seat to make a difference. I acknowledged and explained, ultimately paving the way for us to continue to serve that client and build that relationship even deeper. This, too, was great training in serving senior execs.

There were many meetings and opportunities like that over the course of my corporate career. I considered being part of every one of them an honor. A great caddy doesn't just carry a golfer's bag: They prepare and research. They advise and cajole. They clean and they calculate. They allow that golfer to rest, to practice the right things, and to perform without distractions or excuses. And that's what a great Chief of Staff can do for you. (Although not even a great Chief can help you break 70!)

Crossing the Fence

My Chief of Staff role led me to Texas. And while there's no cowgirl in me, I love it here. It's a wonderful place—one where I enjoy the climate (most months anyway), the convenience of the central time zone, and the sense of space. I think the saying is right—everything is bigger in Texas (especially compared to my NYC apartments!). I think back to my days in New York—and it seems like a lifetime ago. The move to Dallas gave me time to think and reset and find the courage to think even bigger for myself. I knew that as much as I had loved Chiefing, the time had come for a new challenge. A new goal.

Ultimately, I retired (rewired) from my corporate role at AT&T and took all my experiences with me. I show up in the world today serving as a trusted adviser and executive coach to senior executives. *And* I empower a generation of Chiefs of Staff to better serve their own execs. My goal in every instance has been to help people like you reach their fullest expression as a leader by providing them with the support they need—and providing *you* with the support you need. Now, I love that I still get to serve corporate, albeit from a different seat.

I have the honor of working with clients around the globe and across many sectors, and I serve companies of all sizes. I work with new CEOs and founders and C-suite leaders in the F100. The senior executives I serve come with different personalities, capabilities, and dreams. I help these leaders and their Chiefs of Staff build better relationships and perform at the very highest level, together. I've even had clients call me a "Mission Whisperer," and honestly, I kinda like it.

Every time I work with a new client, my insights grow, and I expand my range and abilities as a coach. I am deeply grateful to serve in this way.

What Defines a Great Chief?

We will look at this question in some detail. But the short answer is only three letters long: *you. You* define the Chief who will support you and actualize your vision with exceptional skill. A great Chief gets you. Understands you. Respects you. Serves you. Amplifies you. They make their work entirely relevant to yours and help influence your mission. They see that although you may look calm and controlled from the outside, beneath the surface, that swan may be kicking furiously. You are in constant demand and struggling to prioritize. You need balance. And likely some sleep! They will help you to adapt. To see exactly what is holding you back. To transform your life and unleash your full potential. Renowned leadership expert John C. Maxwell observed that "The pessimist complains about the wind. The optimist expects it to change. The leader adjusts the sails." A great Chief will help you adjust yours and keep you sailing on the course, no matter what kind of storm you're facing.

What Does This Actually Look Like?

The talk about transformation is all well and good—but what does "transformation" mean when you're sitting in your office in the middle of another busy week?

Let's look at Kyle, a client I recently worked with. Kyle is a "type A" perfectionist. I recognized it immediately, as I am an Enneagram 1 with massive perfectionist tendencies. (PS: This trait was a plus when I was a Chief, but if not properly managed, it can really get in my way. I learned that valuable lesson early on!) Kyle was being pulled in every direction. He was responsible for such a high proportion of the company's revenue that he was constantly having to answer to the engine that runs him—also known as "The Board Chair." At 2 a.m., he would still be up working, revising presentations for multiple meetings and preparing to provide regular updates to the board and investors regarding the latest issues.

Without realizing it—without the breathing room to take stock of his situation—Kyle was directing his passion toward the wrong places. He was sitting in on call after call to appear "present" but completely losing sight of his purpose. He spent so much time explaining the work that he had no time to *do* the work. A strong leader (and a great guy), failing for all the right reasons. As the saying goes, the road to hell is paved with good intentions. For Kyle, the intentions were great, but the road was definitely leading in the wrong direction . . .

Enter Sarah. His knight in shining armor. She observed his work week, sat him down, and reminded him that he had been appointed to drive growth and manage thousands of points of distribution. That would require a complete refocus. She took on his calendar and, with masterful prioritization, helped determine who he needed to meet. Every meeting was soon booked through Sarah. The minutiae were redirected. The calendar was cleared so he could focus on his biggest priorities. Within three months, Kyle was taking the business to the places he had promised when he took on the role. That's the impact of Sarah's great Chiefing. (We'll get to see the other side of this story—how he enabled her to succeed—in Chapter 6.)

Admit It: You Need Help!

Not enough time. Information overload. Constant interruptions. Losing sight of the big picture. These common challenges leaders like you face have a simple solution: A Chief of Staff to help turn around the ship. A Chief of Staff who seeks out problems and solves them before they reach your desk. A Chief who becomes your eyes and ears in the organization. A Chief of Staff who anticipates what you need to know and delivers on it. A Chief whose first responsibility is to *you*. One who burrows away getting the dirty work done so you don't have to even know about it. One who unlocks clarity, execution, harmony, and excellence. They prove that the answer isn't a new executive, it's a new approach. Your corporate caddy. As author and motivational speaker Simon Sinek puts it:

"It is like when a player has a slump, we do not trade them, we coach them. It is the same with our employees. The best leaders come to the aid of their people, whose performance is down. Not come down harder on them."

A Weight Lifted

Have you ever worried so long and hard about something that its resolution allows you to feel your shoulders drop? Once again, you're breathing slowly. You wonder how you ever coped before. That's the impact that a great Chief of Staff will have on your life.

Of course, this won't happen by magic. It's mission-critical to find a person whose strengths complement yours. Equally important: you must like and trust each other. Few professional relationships will ever be as intimate as the one between you and your Chief of Staff. The chemistry may be palpable from the start, but you can't develop this full, profound dynamic instantly. With attention and intention, your Chief will become your closest adviser and confidant. They will talk truth to power, provoking you where necessary. You must be able to rely on them completely, to interpret the "silent nod"—based on deep foundations of trust and a shared worldview. It is a kind of alchemy that delivers missions and develops teams. And that's when sh*t gets real.

The Measurable Benefit

Unnecessary problems never reach the surface. Time becomes yours again. Your blind spots disappear. And these changes are only the means to an end, because when you and your Chief of Staff are working in harmony, the sum becomes more than its parts. And your ability to execute is transformed. You become better in your role. And the results will show up in your bottom line. Having a Chief of Staff in your corner lets your ideas land and lets you to have the impact you know you can deliver.

Ready to Read On?

I hope this has whetted your appetite. Does it make you want to go out there right this second and hire a Chief? If so, please slow down! You don't want to get this wrong. Hence, the rest of this book. I want you to find the right person and ignite them in the right way, so that you've set yourself up for long-term success—which, paradoxically, means making your Chief replaceable.

This book is broken into two sections. **In the first section**, we will look at some of your biggest challenges as a leader: unmanaged time, loneliness, problem solving versus preventing, lack of alignment, and a reactive team who finds it easiest to say "yes." And I'll reveal how the right Chief of Staff can extinguish them all (the challenges, not the team!). **The second section** is focused on hiring a Chief of Staff and enabling them to hit the ground running. If you already have a Chief of Staff and the relationship needs work to be more effective, I'll cover that too. I've got you!

You'll see little **boxed stories** throughout the book, too. These are examples from my coaching clients (identifying details have been changed, as with all case studies throughout the book), stories I've included to illustrate the ways your leadership problems can be solved by an effective Chief.

It has been my passion and my honor to help many senior executives clear what they imagine are insurmountable obstacles by engaging an exceptional Chief of Staff. My heart is in this work, in this book, and with you, too, as you find your way to deliver your highest impact as a leader.

You'd be surprised to discover that leaders of all kinds, whether at the very beginning of their career or at huge Fortune100s, are often struggling with the very same challenges you face every day. I know this because I've worked with them, I've coached them, and I've seen them transform with a powerful Chief at their side. I encourage you to take my guidance—and their stories—as a balm. You are not alone, and the answer to your challenges is right here in your hands.

It is my hope that as you make your way through this book, the content will prompt thoughts and reflections about how you can optimize our own business by engaging a highly effective Chief of Staff. With this knowledge, you will be able to take what you have learned and put it into action to create a more efficient and effective work environment.

The number of Chiefs of Staff in nongovernment roles has more than doubled since 2007. In an hour or two, I hope you'll be on the way to joining that lucky group of visionaries. They would concur entirely with Kyle's words from when we met recently:

"Without Sarah as my right hand, I would not have been able to drive the impact that I did for my firm. She's the glue that holds us all together."

Sit back, hit recline, and let's go get you the right Chief of Staff!

CHAPTER 1

How Do I Know *You* Need a Chief of Staff?

Your Executive Emergency Service

I've heard it from so many beleaguered execs: Your inbox is bulging. Scrolling down it feels never-ending. Your desk is piled high with folders that are starting to block your view of the door. Your phone has logged several missed calls and too many voice messages to count. There's a knot in your stomach and your heart seems to be beating a little too fast. In private, you are beginning to really doubt yourself.

You have a helpful assistant. But their role is on the micro side. They can move meetings, book travel, and take messages, but they aren't hired or paid to take the bigger strain.

Do you feel like you're in over your head?

Don't panic. There is a solution. Your new highly effective and life-saving Chief of Staff!

The Evolution of the Chief

Let's look back. This isn't a new idea. It has been tried and tested over millennia. In ancient Rome, many governors or army generals would engage a *Princeps Officii* to manage their day-to-day operations, allowing them to focus on high politics and strategy.

In politics, the Chief of Staff (CoS) has often become something of a legend in his or her own right. Ronald Reagan described his right hand, James A Baker III, in these glowing terms: "As he had demonstrated with the Soviets, Baker recognized that the person across the table had his or her own domestic politics to worry about and he made a point of looking for ways to satisfy those needs while still getting what he wanted."

Leo McGarry in the television series *The West Wing* demonstrated just what it takes to be a great Chief—releasing pressure on the president and "getting things done" while developing and implementing strategies to improve efficiency across the organization. And while he did that, he always had President Bartlet's back.

What fewer people realize is that there is an equally important role for a Chief in nonpolitical organizations. Senior executives are equally weighed down by massive responsibilities and expectations. Getting through all the tasks intact, while leaving time for what really matters, simply isn't something that can be done alone.

Still thinking about the stacks of folders, unaddressed messages, competing demands, lack of resources, keynote prep, upcoming board meeting, *et cetera, et cetera, aaagh!?* Then read on. Once you have a solid grasp of what an effective Chief can do for you, you'll exhale. Promise.

The Power Pair

"I can do things you cannot, you can do things I cannot do.
Together, we can do great things."
– Unknown

This is not merely an outsourcing relationship or an expanded secretarial role, but a professional partnership grounded in deep trust and authenticity. It enables quick decision-making and harmonious collaboration. It's akin to the powerful dynamics between adviser and confidant, pilot and copilot, surgeon and nurse, golfer and caddy. Such trust and authenticity allow the pair to navigate tricky situations swiftly and effectively.

In business, the Chief of Staff keeps an executive organized, focused, and on track. They prioritize the executive's schedule, prepare them for key meetings, manage their time-consuming relationships (from board members to investors), and coordinate cohesive communications—both internal and external. A powerful CEO I once worked with shared that a great Chief of Staff is more of a delegator than a coordinator. He is so right!

An effective Chief of Staff is adept at orchestrating work with and through others. They are the linchpin of the organization, ensuring every component operates in harmony. In short, they hold the keys to organizational success and smooth operation, not just supporting but elevating the team's overall performance.

The Modern-Day Chief Demystified: CoS vs. EA

The modern-day Chief of Staff role is often misunderstood, and that's because it's not a cookie-cutter position.

By definition, each Chief's role will reflect the strengths and needs of the leader they serve. No two leaders are identical. Nor are any two Chiefs.

No two leaders are identical. Nor are any two Chiefs.

A former colleague once tried to sum up the Chief of Staff role as "a glorified Executive Assistant." Truthfully? I took a little offense! Not because I underrate the role of the executive assistant, but because the Chief of Staff position requires a very different skill set.

If you'd like another opinion, the distinction is well-explained by this passage from the *Harvard Business Review*:

"The Chief of Staff role is decidedly different from that of the leader's Executive Assistant (EA). A Chief of Staff works autonomously and does not handle routine correspondence or manage the leader's day-to-day schedule. *The highest-level CoS should be a full-fledged member of the senior leadership team*, albeit without the rank or compensation of a C-suite officer." (Italics mine.)

This diagram by the office food delivery service SnackNation further depicts the differences between the Chief, EA, and the Chief Operating Officer (COO):

OVERARCHING DIFFERENCES BETWEEN EA, CoS, AND COO

	EA	CoS	COO
Operating Method	Tactical and organizational acumen	Upbeat, direct, efficiency driver	Foresight combined with strategic presence
Primary Objective	Ensure everything gets done	Alignment, progress, leadership	Keep business running most efficiently and effectively
Regularly Involved In	Keep meetings productive and efficient	Developing company-wide communication and correspondence	Coaching or collaborating with functional heads
Mantra	"Leave no task unfinished."	"Let's be clear."	"Always right and has the job title to prove it."
Authority	Most apparent when acting on CEO's behalf	Unmistakable, but unofficial	Oversees the majority of resources
Necessary Evil	Managing email inboxes	Monitoring department goals and metrics	Addresses underperforming groups

© SnackNation, 2023

Relieving the Burden

What does this mean on the ground? One of the CEOs I had the honor of Chiefing for said the Chief *and* EA were 100% essential to his success. As his Chief, I was his right hand, and his EA was his left. He could not do without either of us. The three of us had a powerful working relationship that enabled our CEO to focus on his top priorities and drive high impact.

A great Chief of Staff can:

- Oversee a combination of strategy and operations across your business.

- Generate order from chaos.

- Create efficiencies so you can prioritize what really matters and lead with your strengths.

- Lead and direct with authority.

- Serve you without needing to please you. (No, they are not the same.)

- Cover your blind spots.

- Provide advice and counsel as your trusted ally and adviser.

And word is getting out that Chiefs of Staff are crucial to leadership in the business world. Matt Mochary, a top CEO coach and author of *The Great CEO Within*, says the Chief of Staff is the most leveraged hire you can make. "It's so critical, and it's been so successful with all the CEOs that I coach," says Mochary, "that I now require it before I coach somebody."

Guess What? There's Research!

Much of what I have written in these pages is based on my concrete experience. "It just works!" But current data also confirms what our intuition tells us. The latest research on Secure Base Leadership theory suggests we all need people in our lives who "have our backs."

Furthermore, attachment theory explains that we are biologically wired to seek out social connections and form attachments with others. Only when we feel safe and secure in our relationships are we able to thrive and reach our full potential.

This scientific insight has implications for how we think about leadership more broadly. It's not just leaders who thrive in a climate of safety and security. So do their teams. It's crucial that people can understand how to be themselves, voice their opinions, and take risks without fear of repercussions.

It may sound simple, but the workplace can be an intimidating, transactional environment. Great leaders need their teams to feel like a part of the mission. And a great Chief can be exactly the right catalyst to make this happen.

OCTAVIO *before* DAVE

Octavio had a sharp vision and ceaseless determination. He had a start-up idea he was sure would change the cellular phone landscape. He jumped the hurdles, established his business, and launched to massive fanfare. But while fanfare is pretty exciting, it also doubles the stress and worry that an entrepreneur experiences when they're taking their vision all the way. Teeming with stress and doubting he could ever stay on top of his unending torrent of tasks, he secretly slept at the office more nights than not. Octavio had thought success would feel beautiful, but this? This just felt brutal. He needed to share the burden.

OCTAVIO *after* DAVE

Octavio would never have considered a Chief of Staff, because Octavio didn't know they were "a thing." In fact, when an acquaintance stopped Octavio in the parking lot to introduce Octavio to his new Chief of Staff, his response was: "Your new what?"

Within a month, Octavio had hired Dave. Whip-smart, experienced, and comfortable in his skin, Dave became Octavio's most trusted ally. Their working partnership rapidly advanced the success of the company, increasing revenues and expanding the size and range of the team, allowing Octavio to build what he describes as "a beautiful life" outside the office.

The Missing Piece

We may not have met yet, but I know how challenging your job is. I understand how isolating, overwhelming, and anxiety-inducing it can be to lead. As you strive to make the biggest impact possible on your company and the people you support, I want to tell you that your Chief of Staff is downright *essential* to your success.

Together, you and your Chief of Staff can create an environment where team members feel safe and supported to do their best work.

A Chief can:

- Assist you by providing honest feedback, keeping track of your deadlines and commitments, and managing day-to-day operations.

- Free you up to focus on creating your company's healthiest climate and culture.

- Act as a sounding board and challenger, providing you with a safe space to brainstorm and think through difficult decisions.

The highly skilled, well-trained person who holds this position can help you transform your company and, by extension, your life. When the relationship works, your visions and dreams will—almost immediately—become a step closer to reality.

If You Have a Little Time, Try Out the Exercises in This Book. *Really!*

To manifest a profound shift in your approach to serving as a senior executive, I urge you to consider where you are and where you want to go. No doubt you are practiced at thinking through the changes you can make to advance your business. I challenge you to apply those same executive skills to reflect on the changes you need for *your* sake—for both your professional success and your personal happiness.

So, at the end of each chapter in this book, you will find a series of questions that relate to what you've just read. Take out a pen and a notebook, and give the prompts your attention. And hold onto your notes afterward. They may help you evaluate, monitor, and adjust your progress down the line.

Believe me when I say this won't be time wasted. The clearer you are about where you need to go and what's blocking your way, the more quickly you will find yourself on the other side—the desk clear, the electronic backlog eliminated, your inbox (and your insides) ready for what's next.

By asking and reflecting on these questions, you can gain a deeper understanding of the kind of support you need to be successful in your role.

Jot down answers to these questions. Trust what emerges on the page, especially if your responses surprise you. When your thinking isn't ambling down well-trodden paths, you're being guided by your subconscious. That's you, discovering what you didn't know you knew!

Take a few minutes. Free and easy. Then we can move on!

Exercise

1. What kind of support do I yearn for in my position as a leader?

2. What are the biggest challenges that I currently face as a leader, and what kind of support would help me overcome these challenges?

3. How do I define success in my role as a leader, and what kind of support do I need to achieve that success?

4. What are my biggest strengths and weaknesses as a leader?

CHAPTER 2

The Four Meta Problems

Your Personal Problem Solver

My client Nick manufactures clever gifts for animal lovers. He is super smart and innovative. His business has grown exponentially thanks to his great ideas and work ethic. He wanted to scale up his business, but when we met, he just felt that a Chief of Staff wasn't for him. It was something for a senior politician or an established corporate CEO. Nick saw himself as scrappy, driven, and self-sufficient.

I explained that he was in the perfect position to benefit from the magic of a Chief. Someone who could take the strain and grow with Nick and the company. Shortly thereafter, he hired Nicole and asked me to coach her to peak performance.

Nicole and I met regularly over six months. We designed plans for her to establish a solid operating rhythm, build trust with the leadership team, and drive accountability with the functional heads. Ultimately, these objectives all built toward a single goal: to serve Nick and his mission.

It wasn't all smooth sailing. Some days, Nicole needed a sounding board to work through a murky situation. On others, she sought help recommending options to Nick as he was making critical decisions for the firm. We covered it all.

The results she helped achieve were amazing. In a matter of months, with Nick's support, the company saw improved employee engagement, built a healthy culture, established an A+ leadership team, and helped the extended leadership team improve their performance across all fronts. I felt like a proud mom whose child has just come home from school with top grades!

Nick's life was transformed. "Without Nicole as my right hand, I would not have been able to drive the impact that I did for my firm," he explained. "She's the glue that holds us all together." After a year as Chief of Staff, Nicole was promoted to the role of Vice President of Business Operations. His company is still thriving.

What Can a Chief Do for You?

A great Chief of Staff can revolutionize the quality of an executive's work. And that revolution grows directly from the strength of the relationship between Leader and Chief.

Do any of the following challenges resonate with you?

- Struggling to reach your full expression in leadership.
- Failing to drive meaningful contributions to your customers, employees, and shareholders.
- Questioning your critical decision-making.
- Spending too long absent from your zone of genius.

- Worrying about how to navigate tough turns.

- Sensing your leadership team is operating at less than 100%.

- Feeling that you are not being challenged or stretched.

- Becoming distracted from solutions, innovation, growth, and scaling.

A Chief could become a catalyst for change in all of these areas. Having a Chief is the professional equivalent of not just having your laundry done for you—clean and folded every morning (without you having to ask)—but also getting up to find someone has chosen a great outfit for you, ready to wear, with the hole in your jacket mended before you even knew it existed.

Think of how that would set you on course for your day, how much mental space it would clear for you to explore and manifest the things that matter to you.

Again, this is all supported by the evidence. In the 2020 *Harvard Business Review* article, "The Case for a Chief of Staff," author Dan Ciampa shares that a former CEO who now advises boards argues that many chief executives need a Chief of Staff to help the office function smoothly. Additionally, a 2018 survey of hundreds of CEOs from around the world conducted by the consulting firm Egon Zehnder provides compelling insight into the biggest challenges facing CEOs, supporting what I've seen all along. The top problems senior leaders share often sound like this:

- I've got too much to do and not enough time.

- I'm overwhelmed by information.

- I'm constantly interrupted.

- I have difficulty making decisions.

- I suffer paralysis through analysis.

- I'm second-guessing myself.

- I'm losing sight of the big picture.

- I'm being pulled in too many directions.

- I'm failing to delegate.

- I'm micromanaging.

Combining the research with my firsthand experience as a Chief of Staff and the confessions and exasperations I've heard from Chiefs of Staff and the high-level executives I've coached, I have identified four meta problems that seem to afflict those in leadership positions.

The Four Meta Problems

"Life is a like a box of chocolates," explained Forrest Gump on that park bench. "You never know what you're gonna get." It's the very same for problems, only they don't just sit in a box. They can fly toward you at a dizzying pace. They show up in different shapes and sizes, and you can't predict which one is coming at you next. If you've spent more than one day in a C-suite position, you know what I'm describing. And you know how stressful it can be to keep up with it all.

Throughout my years of Chiefing and coaching leaders, I made it my primary goal to define and prioritize problem-solving. I won't regale you with all my findings, though, because the headline is simple: There are four common meta problems that can derail an executive. These problems can dominate your life, distract you from what matters, and cause high levels of stress. They are the great white sharks within your business—not always evident, but lurking under the surface nonetheless, ready to rear their heads at the worst possible moment.

A great Chief will help keep the water safe, and deal with those sharks when they make an unwanted appearance.

Meta Problem 1: My Time Is Totally Unmanaged

When time ceases to be your friend, you are in trouble. Stress replaces clear thinking. Rushing replaces consideration. You create a treadmill effect—running faster but standing still. Slowly, you get ground down. Exhaustion means you are less productive. Overcommitment kills energy.

I like to use the terms *time* and *energy* interchangeably because they are intrinsically linked.

Well-managed time means ample available energy, and vice versa. In contrast, having dwindling energy as a leader will ultimately take a toll on your mental and physical health while damaging the company's bottom line.

| Well-managed time means ample available energy.

Meta Problem 2: It's Lonely at the Top

The further you rise up the corporate ladder, the less accessible you become. This is not necessarily by choice. People are respectful of leaders. They are also inhibited in their presence—and that's often not a good thing. That inhibition can become a barrier to honest feedback and empathy. Not many employees ask the boss if they're feeling okay or if they fancy a quick drink.

No wonder so many people in leadership roles say they feel isolated, anxious, and depressed.

Meta Problem 3: My Team Spends More Time Solving Problems Versus Preventing Them

Albert Einstein observed that "Intellectuals solve problems, geniuses prevent them." In business life, that adage needs adapting: hard workers solve problems, great teams prevent them.

> ### "Intellectuals solve problems, geniuses prevent them."

I never cease to be frustrated at how much time leaders waste solving problems that could have been avoided. It's like watching someone forget to switch off the faucet and then have to spend days cleaning out the flooded bathroom.

So often, the problem is caused by leaders being too busy to develop a sixth sense of where the next leak is coming from. As a result, the pressure stacks up while the leader expends much too much time fixing things.

Meta Problem 4: I'm Surrounded by "Yes" People

You want a debate, and you get a roomful of nods. You want creativity, but you get affirmation. It might sound nice, but it isn't healthy. Organizations only move forward when their culture fosters ideas, innovation, and constructive criticism. A star leader whom people only follow timidly is not a great leader at all.

In my experience, this "yes" environment flourishes because of the leader, not the team. A leader too busy to be accessible, with no time to take the temperature of the wider group, will become disengaged and isolated.

The Throughline: Misalignment

There is a common thread weaving through all of these meta problems, and that's a lack of alignment among and between your leaders and functions. Great teams share a mission and a sense of purpose and direction. When those elements are absent, teams struggle.

In every case of a struggling leader, I have found misalignment. It is often linked to communication, be it an absence of clarity around the mission, a lack of interaction between leader and team, or a culture that stops feedback from making its way back to the top. Whatever the cause, an absence of alignment is invariably the trouble the leader must resolve.

Luckily, a Chief of Staff has alignment in their sights from the start. Indeed, alignment is central to their core mission. And, as you'll see in the coming chapters, the Chief's skill with achieving it can knock the four meta problems out at their source.

Take a Moment to Reflect

We will, of course, explore the meta problems in detail. Each can be solved with a Chief of Staff in tow. At this point, I ask you to take a moment to consider what you have read so far. How many of these meta problems are significant challenges in your life as a leader?

My years in this field have shown me that leaders of all kinds—from those most visibly successful to those in the rough-and-tumble early stages of their executive lives—struggle with these issues. The meta problems come with the territory, and unless you were born knowing how to make miracles, you are likely to encounter them.

Exercise

1.   Take five minutes and jot down any problems or challenges you're having in your position as leader. Let it all spill out. Only you will read this. Big issues, small ones—purge! Write fast—that's the best way for the subconscious to unload (and it saves time!).

2.   Pause before taking another five minutes. Then, dive back in. This time, write out a list of everything you can imagine that would make up your perfect working day. What do you yearn to feel and experience as you lead your organization? What does the vulnerable, distressed, exhausted voice in you say it needs? If all fails with that approach, the next couple of questions can serve as prompts to spark your thinking a bit.

3.   Reflect on how you allocate your time and whether you are maximizing your productivity. Are you effectively managing your time and priorities?

4.   Do you feel you can delegate effectively, or is delegating a challenge for you?

CHAPTER 3

Meta Problem 1:
My Time Is Completely Unmanaged

"I must govern the clock, not be governed by it."
– Golda Meir

Meet Kent. The ultimate swan.

What his colleagues saw was an exceptional C-suite leader. A man of action: driving strong impact, delivering results. The board loved him, and his team respected him. He took pride in making himself available for anyone in his network who needed support one-on-one.

His desire to accommodate played havoc with his calendar, because if someone needed a favor, a fact, or a file checked, he always said yes. Like a 21st-century George Bailey from *It's a Wonderful Life*, he put everyone else first.

Kent never let anyone down. Except for one person: himself. A lovely, middle-aged man . . . who'd had a heart attack the year before we met. He had spent years putting himself under far, far too much strain—a strain that was always increasing, as his own goals and commitments were pushed further and further back by his efforts to help everyone he could.

When he hired me as his executive coach, I saw what was going on under the surface: A man paddling so furiously that he never stopped. Whose desire to accommodate everybody had left him stretched thin and stressed beyond measure.

When we met, I saw a man whose honesty, work ethic, and ambitious drive had led him to the point of complete exhaustion. I could see it on his face. He explained that he had back pain at night. He had stopped exercising (against doctor's orders) because he was worried that time at the gym was eating into his working day. His claim was that there were not enough hours in the day to dedicate to his health. Seriously.

As you can probably tell, Kent had a major problem: His time had become completely unmanaged. And the results were, quite literally, killing him.

Kent and I worked together for several months. We agreed that he needed to create firm boundaries guiding his use of time and energy. We agreed that he needed more impact from less effort. We agreed that he needed to preserve his energy and health, and that he wasn't prepared to sacrifice his career to do so.

And then we got to work on the ultimate game of calendar management. In Chapter One, we looked at how a great Chief of Staff differs from a great Executive Assistant; Kent's story is the perfect illustration. We didn't simply move appointments around or create more empty hours. That seemed too obvious.

We prioritized his time to align for the big things—the initiatives that were most important to him and the ones that would drive the most impact. We discussed what could realistically be delegated, and in some cases, what could be deleted or dismissed completely. We mapped his input against his impact.

And after all that? Kent survived. More than that, Kent flourished. His time became more structured. His efforts were more measured. His calendar was more streamlined. He had been suffering from time mismanagement. The cure was quite simple: hire a Chief of Staff who understood and helped him share the burden. And moving forward, he did just that.

Stop the Madness!

Enough about Kent. Let's talk about you. And if you have read this far, I'm going to make a few educated guesses:

Your job is made up of many moving parts. You receive an almost endless stream of requests and demands, all competing for your attention. When it's not a stream, it's a tidal wave.

In-house, you attend board meetings, town halls, skip levels and listening tours, staff meetings, project updates, and more.

Externally, you have keynotes, panels, fireside chats, and investor meetings in the calendar—not to mention a few pitches and meetings that you've been asked to attend without any clear reason why.

Every time you look at the calendar, you feel needed and at the very center of the corporate world. But you also feel daunted. You may even feel panicked. After all, once all those meetings are done, and you've read the follow-up material and answered all the subsequent correspondence, you must start thinking about your actual job!

You're a leader. You have a strategy to build. A team to lead. A whole set of goals to reach. And a high impact to deliver. Eyes are on you. You feel the pressure from your clients, employees, and shareholders. But you also want to be the perfect boss. The perfect colleague.

So, you start to make choices to enable you to fit it all in. You get up earlier and leave later. You skip meals and replace them with snacks. You go to bed exhausted, and if you're lucky enough to sleep, you still wake up tired. You work weekends and evenings. You sacrifice family time to manage your inbox. Even when you're present around the people you love, you're not there. You guzzle caffeine and dream of a vacation. Slowly but surely, you grow closer and closer to burnout.

The irony is that nobody is actually benefiting from your insane level of effort. The more you work, the less effective you are at your job. Gradually, the single, overriding reason you were appointed in the first place becomes a mere afterthought.

JED *before* TONI

Jed had finally landed the CEO position and the corner office that went with it. When younger-Jed imagined the life of a CEO, he thought he'd spend most of his time admiring the view from that office. But once he was actually there, he hardly ever had time to glance out the window. His responsibilities were massive, and he was drowning but ashamed to ask for help. He had no idea how to organize his days so he could clear enough mental space to think through his work, much less settle in and enjoy what he'd fought all those years to achieve.

JED *after* TONI

Jed knew about Chiefs of Staff from politics and TV. He had no idea there could be one for him in his position. Now, he says, Toni was the best hire he ever made. Fiercely smart with a playbook of moves that would change his working life, she showed up ready to carve his schedule free from the million tasks he didn't need to be focusing on. She took care of everything that didn't truly need his attention, and as a result, he made more and more of a difference as a leader. The gift he values the most is that he finally had time to get to know his team on a personal level—and that brought the whole company together.

Govern the Clock

You know the problem. And you also know the solution. You just can't quite admit it. Something must give. And that's your calendar. You need to be wiser with your time. Without that control, nothing else works.

Meet Your Fairy Time Manager!

In a fairy tale, there's a moment when, at peak crisis, the Fairy Godmother appears quite magically and gets to work. She waves her wand, rearranges what seemed fixed in place, and creates resources and possibilities where before there was nothing but disappointment. This allows a stressed and upset Cinderella to get to the ball with minimal anxiety.

Your corporate equivalent is a Chief of Staff. This magical guide understands your business, your priorities, and, most importantly, you. They have the power to remove the dead weight from your calendar. To give you the luxury of time. Quickly, effectively, and permanently. Even if they lose a whole bunch of their own time in the process.

And This Is How They'll Do It

Your Chief will step back and map your goals and responsibilities against your calendar. Let's call him Steve. He'll ensure you have enough time simply to think, without being judged or pressured. You don't need to worry about how he does it, but if you're interested, it'll be through a thorough process of reprioritization in alignment with your key goals. You'll suddenly find that a bunch of meetings have disappeared. Quietly, but crucially, Steve will attend to them on your behalf, filtering out the waste and briefing you only on what you need to know.

> **You get to spend vital periods of the day in your zone of genius.**

This is more than a time-saving exercise. It's pivotal. Having your time managed effectively frees you to do what you do best. You get to spend vital periods of the day in your zone of genius, while the world around you continues to evolve. Effectively, Steve is releasing your creativity from captivity.

Your Chief of Staff: Protecting Your Time

Once your Chief has helped you fight the initial fire, you will feel your shoulders drop as your anxiety levels fall. That's when your Chief can move into an organizational mode, dealing with your gargantuan to-do list and the many people howling for your attention. They will probably do it like this:

Prioritize by Importance

Work with you to identify your most important goals—individually and for your team. Map those against your calendar. Ensure you are only present when it matters.

Prioritize by the Deadline

Clarify what's needed urgently and what can wait. Anything that is crucial and immediate rises to the top of your pile. You'll never again see anything low priority or nonurgent. Think of the mental space that will open for you. And the increased space to focus on your top priorities.

Delegation

You know delegation matters, but it probably worries you. Will others do the job inadequately? Will you lose control? Will you end up with more work? Not when you have a great Chief of

Staff by your side. They will scrutinize every piece of delegated work. They will understand your standards and your concerns. They'll turn ad hoc delegation into a process that is carefully managed and nurtured.

Learning to Say "No"

I'm going to guess that you've developed a dangerous "yes" habit. You are genuinely trying to help. And your self-image swells every time your "yes" leads to success. But you've dug yourself into a hole. When you are too busy lending a hand, you cease to be good at what you're paid for. Your Chief of Staff will help you say no. They will set boundaries. Divert requests before they reach you. Saying "no" is difficult. It is also an invaluable time-management skill. When you say "no" to one thing, you say "yes" to something else.

| Your Chief of Staff will help you say no.

Embracing your "default no" doesn't make you a negative person. It makes you a sensible leader. There will, of course, be times you need to fight your own fires, attend urgent meetings, and get distracted by something appropriately important. But these incidents need to be exceptions. Your Chief of Staff will keep you informed, engaged, and accountable to your promises. They will also help you say "no" in the right way. Or they'll just say it for you!

Coordinating

A great Executive Assistant can block your calls, move your appointments, and allow you to breathe. A great Chief of Staff has that extra superpower of representing you, managing on your behalf, and coordinating your work.

At the moment, effective coordination of the people and projects you lead may not be happening at all. Or, you may be the one trying to handle all the coordinating, even though you've got your share of other responsibilities screaming for your attention.

The coordination of separate teams and workstreams is priceless. It streamlines your work while creating a whole that is more than the sum of its parts. It can drive different areas toward goals that you suddenly have the time to engineer. And it can let you breathe.

Exercise

1. Grab your notebook.

2. Think back to a moment when you felt pulled in a million directions. When you were busy every moment but not actually achieving anything. What was the situation? Who was involved? What was at stake?

3. How did you feel? What did you do to cope?

4. How could the kind of support I've described in this section have helped?

5. What would you do with all the time and space you get back?

CHAPTER 4

Meta Problem 2:
It's Lonely at the Top

*"Ironically, the higher I climbed the corporate ladder, the more I felt the
weight of isolation. Being a CEO is an incredibly lonely journey, where the
air thins as you ascend, and the silence becomes deafening."*
— Indra Nooyi, former CEO of PepsiCo

When Abraham Lincoln recommended, "Avoid popularity
if you would have peace," he could have had Marilyn
in mind.

Marilyn is a dazzling, groundbreaking, wildly popular CEO in
the social media space. You may know her (but not as Marilyn,
of course). She's regularly featured in magazines and reputable
publications. As a powerful influencer, she's invited to keynotes
that people actually listen to. She creates a strong impression
and even stronger numbers. Her team loves her almost as much
as her investors do. In short, she's a star.

Her star has always shone brightly on the outside. Marilyn appeared at work with grace and a smile. She radiated positive energy that was contagious to all in her orbit. This created a snowball effect, and demand for Marilyn kept growing. Everyone wanted her time and her dynamism. More and more and more.

That all sounds good, right? Well . . . not so fast!

Very few people see an actor between performances. The queen without her crown. Nobody saw Marilyn away from the spotlight. So, nobody saw her alone.

Nobody saw that she was deeply lonely and depressed. Down. Unsupported. She had the ability to armor up for the working day, but behind the scenes, she desperately wanted to slow her pace, take stock, and be more strategic with her time and energy.

Marilyn wanted to run the show, but she'd found herself caught in the performance. Have you ever felt this way?

Saving Marilyn

Fortunately, Marilyn reached out to me. I began by asking her some questions aimed at taking an inventory of her support circle.

"Who are your reliable confidants?" I asked. "Do you have a trusted sounding board?" "Who would you consider to be your personal board of directors?"

Can you imagine where this is going? This charismatic, popular, and dynamic leader couldn't come up with a single person. She knew almost everyone but didn't consider any of them "intimate." In a time of stress, there was nobody she knew who had her back or would give her a second opinion she valued—really valued—and needed!

So, it was clear where we had to start. We had to create a squad of people around her who were briefed and able to support, question, and most importantly, challenge her. She desperately needed someone to share the burden, or at least make her feel less alone. People whose very existence could counter the excruciating sense of loneliness that haunted her away from the front line.

Who Has Your Back?

It's always been tough at the top. But today's business environment is tougher than ever. Creating an efficient team and working seamlessly between its constituent parts is ever more challenging. The pressure to be inclusive, accepting, and empathetic is constant. There is so much to do, particularly when the ability to walk through the office saying hello has been replaced by dozens of individual Zoom calls.

As a leader, you are up at the top of that tree, where there's much more to do and with very little support. You may be solitary, physically, which can add to the sense of loneliness and separation. This kind of isolation can contribute to what I call "CEO Impostor Syndrome": when your imagination runs wild and your insecurities kick in. This leaves you doubting your own abilities and worrying that you don't deserve to inhabit your role.

And there's a common pattern here. The more time you spend away from your team, the more time you spend doubting your own impact and ability. It's challenging enough meeting your goals, but the constant worry about your productivity and success can be literally exhausting.

You can't keep doing this on your own—at the office or away from it. You need someone who sees you, gets you, and can share the load.

AMY *before* REGINA

Amy had just come home from a gala where she'd been honored as one of the year's top women in business. But her mind was filled with the next day's load of responsibilities. The workload wasn't what was bothering her, though. The higher she'd climbed, the more isolated she'd become. She had fewer and fewer peers. Now that she was CEO, there was nobody to be absolutely real with. No one to brainstorm with. And no one to celebrate the hard-earned wins with. She was doing a great job. But she felt very alone.

AMY *after* REGINA

Amy knew she needed a Chief and she was open to change. Her search began. She'd seen a number of high-powered candidates, but none of them felt right. Regina was another story. Immediately, they were building on each other's jokes, nodding their heads feverishly about the same likes and dislikes. Had they met at a dinner party, they would have become immediate friends. As it turned out, they were immediate sisters in arms, exchanging ideas and coming up with strategies to manifest Amy's visions. With Regina as Chief of Staff, the company thrived, and Amy was surprised to find herself looking forward to work every day.

Enter Your Chief of Staff

When it comes to this very real—and increasingly common—sense of loneliness, no colleague can make a difference the way a Chief of Staff can.

Your Chief will challenge you without undermining you. They will empathize with you. Be honest with you. Offer advice that you can use. Your Chief is just as committed to your mission and success as you are. Your Chief can do all that because they're not in competition with you. Your priorities are their priorities. And they are the only person at your company whose explicit role is to be absolutely up-front with you. At all times and in all ways.

Tackling Your Sense of Isolation

Your Chief has something very important that you clearly lack—time. And they can use it to:

Connect you with other leaders who also lack the support they need. Reaching out in person and online, your Chief can prepare a network of leaders to help you amplify your thinking and enable you to be even more impactful than you already are.

Schedule team check-ins on topics away from the traditional work agenda. To celebrate achievements, share concerns, offer praise, and develop a spirit of candor and unity. In this way, both you and your team can enjoy the varied forms of human connection everyone wants—and, frankly, needs.

Make time for you to refresh and recharge outside the office. To pursue your hobbies, attend your kid's school events, and make the most of your vacation time. The impact on your perspective can be immense.

Chief to Chief

When you have a Chief of Staff, you have an ally. A sounding board and a strategic thinker. An implementer with creative ideas. Your Chief knows the inner workings of your business and its people. They know your strengths and weaknesses and are prepared to hold up a mirror to you when necessary. They share your burden and understand what's holding you back or getting you down.

When you have a Chief of Staff, you have an ally.

The result is simple: No longer are you alone with your responsibilities. You have a partner at your side.

They say that a problem shared is a problem halved. In my experience, that's an understatement.

The Bridge

When I was a Chief of Staff, I knew that one of my most valuable duties was invisible. It was to take the temperature of the team. To get a sense of how they were feeling (in contrast to how they were performing).

One reason it's lonely at the top is that people tend to keep quiet when the boss walks into the room. The Chief of Staff is far less intimidating. So, those chats by the coffee machine and the water cooler continued, giving me valuable insights into the "real" mood.

It's also a strange truth that people were often much more open with me than they were with my executives, even though they knew that I'd be reporting back. I took advantage of that and was often able to help quell disappointment before it spread.

I also ran "pulse" surveys in conjunction with my HR partner. These captured the team's feelings more quantitatively. My input meant that the surveys included questions whose answers would be directly useful to my leader, requiring no translation or equivocation.

The collective result of this work meant my leader was never caught by surprise. He had time to prepare answers—or even to solve problems—before issues reached him. We tailored communication to suit the audiences and even arranged for him to make "impromptu" visits to the local market office hubs to engage with people I sensed needed some attention and support. The outcome was satisfying for all involved.

Think about how this could benefit you. A bridge between the boardroom and the shop floor. An ability to judge with certainty the "real" feelings among your team. An opportunity to create a healthy ecosystem based on knowledge rather than instinct.

Ultimately, having a Chief of Staff connects you to your team. So much of that feeling of "loneliness" is about not knowing. About feeling isolated and in the dark. In that sense, a great Chief of Staff really can switch the lights back on.

Ask Sally

Okay, you can't ask Sally. Not in the least because that's not her real name! But Sally is one of the best Chiefs I have ever coached.

She is one of those incredible people who has a sixth sense. She could smell a problem long before it germinated. Nothing ever caught her off guard. And she was so able that she solved the majority of challenges long before Jack, her CEO, had an inkling they existed.

This service didn't stop at specific challenges. Sally routinely took the temperature of the entire workplace. She listened and counseled and knew just when Jack would have to step in personally.

As a result, he never performed better, and his team never felt more valued or part of a more positive culture. Empowered by the information Sally provided, and the trust he had in her, Jack developed real, meaningful, and robust relationships with his leadership team—and their direct reports as well. Talk about blasting through the loneliness of the unknown!

Exercise

Freewrite about your experience of loneliness or isolation in your work situation. Here are some prompts to get you started:

1. Do you ever feel lonely or isolated in your position? If so, when and in what context?

2. What might the causes of your loneliness be? Dig deep.

3. How do you typically cope with feelings of loneliness or isolation? Are there any strategies that have been particularly effective for you?

4. Are there any specific aspects of your role that contribute to feelings of loneliness or isolation? For example, do you feel disconnected from your employees, or do you struggle to find peers who understand the unique challenges of your role?

5. How would your life change if something (or someone) could make all your problems disappear?

CHAPTER 5

Meta Problem 3:
My Team Is Solving Problems, Not Preventing Them

"An ounce of prevention is worth a pound of cure."

— Benjamin Franklin

Meet Trent, a Frustrated Executive

I'd like to tell you about Trent. Trent was always a great salesman. Give him a target and he'd meet it every time. Raise the bar and he'd clear it. And he was promoted in line with his success. When we met, he was running a huge national sales operation. Being a former sales leader myself, you can imagine we hit it off at hello.

At face value, he appeared to be the right person for the job. He carried himself well and spoke like a true leader. He had a strong and enviable track record of success, and his team saw a man who knew how to handle responsibility.

And yet something was wrong. The teams around him were clearly not at ease in his company. Instead, it was obvious that they walked on eggshells and were constantly worried about his reaction. The department seemed busy with their busy-ness. Trent himself was constantly racing between challenges, but unfortunately, the team's output seemed to be quite a bit less than the sum of its parts. It was like a star-studded basketball team failing to win a single game.

Trent was aware there was a problem but couldn't identify the cause. He was so excited to attend his quarterly offsite meeting where his team would celebrate a big win, but when the time came, he found himself feeling irritable and frustrated.

Trent's Problem

I knew that to get to the roots of this, I needed to do more than talk with Trent. I observed him working. I saw how he addressed every problem the team was facing, jumping between them and ensuring that each team member had his personal attention. It was exhausting for *me*. I can only imagine how it felt for him.

I also saw at close quarters his frustration at the sluggish pace that his top initiatives were moving. It was like his teams were driving with a handbrake on, and for no reason that was apparent to him.

What Trent hadn't realized was that he was that handbrake. He had become so hands-on, so keen to be a visible leader, and so short with those who couldn't live up to his standards, that his direct reports team had lost their own sense of independence and energy.

Moreover, he was spending so long fixing their issues that he had lost his sense of perspective. Trent's lack of clarity was playing out among the members of his team. Each of his direct reports had a different interpretation of the overall company mission. The strategy was being suffocated by detail. Trent had become a fire-fighter when his team needed a real leader. Exhaustion understood.

Repositioning Trent

Trent's entire working life was begging for an overhaul. And he knew it. We built a full-blown war room to take stock of all the challenges absorbing his energy and attention.

Having clear sight of it all was a big step forward for him. Trent instantly understood that he had to delegate. I corrected him and suggested he "gets to" delegate. I wanted him to recognize that delegating does not mean giving away your power. This is something to work on in yourself: always think of delegation as a privilege you "get to do," not a chore you "have to do."

Trent assigned a case manager to solve each challenge from end to end. They were also asked to look at root causes so the team could build prevention measures. It's much harder to put out fires than to stop lighting the candles that start them. This concept was a game changer for Trent. I then challenged him to figure out where else in his life he could strengthen his delegation muscles.

> **It's much harder to put out fires than to stop lighting the candles that start them.**

Delegation gave Trent some very real thinking space. It was clear that he needed to step back and address the company's focus at his next town hall, reiterating the company mission and its role in getting there. He then spoke individually with each of his direct reports to align their work with the mission. This made them feel trusted and valued. Home run, Trent.

The effects were almost instant. A more thoughtful, calmer, and happier Trent. A happier, more aligned team. A healthier environment in which to work.

An Ounce of Prevention

Let's take a look at the world of sports. We grow up surrounded by stories of heroics. The football quarterback who threw a bomb to the wide receiver to win the game. The sprinter who pushed herself to the limit in the last leg of the relay to get the gold for her team.

These stories always place the star in the center of the action. As do movies about extraordinary bravery in battle, or even the moon landing. I am a major movie buff, so I see this all the time. The hero is always Neil Armstrong, not Gene Kranz, the steady and trusted flight director in charge at Mission Control.

As a result, we grow up with a slightly false impression of leadership. Because for all the glory of the hands-on, action-hungry leadership style we crave on screen, businesses thrive on vision and strategy. Every business is full of problem fixers. But great leaders guide strategy. They build strong teams. They prevent problems. The result? They drive strong impact.

JESSICA *before* BILLY

Jessica had actually signed her emails to friends and family back home with the words "Sleepless in Seattle." She had meant it to be funny, but it wasn't. As a senior exec for a multinational technical corporation, Jessica spent virtually every waking moment handling emergencies at work. When she finally got finished with her job, she spent her nights staring at the ceiling fan, spinning with work anxieties. She'd been proud to earn this high-powered position, and she wasn't scared of hard work. But she knew something had to change. Enter Billy . . .

JESSICA *after* BILLY

Jessica's search for the right Chief of Staff was exhaustive. But it also set her back—because everything she didn't get done while she was on the hunt for her CoS was piling up. She needn't have worried, though. Jessica found the person she came to call her "earth angel." That's how she described Billy, her new Chief of Staff, in emails that eased her loved ones' minds. When Billy arrived, everything changed. Billy worked with the team to troubleshoot and tackle issues before they grew into real trouble. Concerns Jessica didn't need to know about never made it to her desk. And her ceiling fan spinning circles in the dark? She wasn't staring at it anymore. She was happily snoring.

How to Add the Most Value to Your Team

Do you crave time to focus on the big picture, but find yourself mired in details? Do you jump from problem to problem, frequently showing your face as a way to demonstrate leadership, only to realize you have little to show for it at the end of the week? Should this model of highly involved leadership be your priority, or should you leave more things to your team and instead get high-level updates on progress?

This is where I strongly suggest a Chief of Staff. Yes, it's amazing how many questions come up with exactly that answer!

At the core, a Chief of Staff is a proactive individual. They are out there on your behalf, scanning for signs of complications, disputes, and other concerns that could erupt into bigger problems. When they spot an issue, they act quickly to neutralize it. They can implement processes and policies to head off trouble before it starts. They do this all day long, but you won't even see it, because a great Chief makes it invisible to you.

At the core, a Chief of Staff is a proactive individual.

This will immediately shield you from unnecessary messes, clearing your time—and your mind—to focus on your high-level obligations. Your Chief will occasionally unearth a challenge that requires your direct intervention. A chance for you to be visible and impactful in a way that adds real value. But in general, your Chief will be able to keep trouble at bay, so you can concentrate on your top priorities.

They say in medicine that prevention is far more powerful than a cure. Think, for instance, how many lives have been saved and treatments avoided because we banned smoking in offices and the workplace. Your Chief performs similar preventive miracles, allowing you to focus your attention where it matters most.

Gimme Some Truth

Knowledge is power. But too often, it can be the person at the top who is the last to receive important information. Perhaps it's because team members find the leader intimidating. Or people assume the leader is too busy. In many cases, everyone imagines the person on top must already be aware.

Whatever the reason, a senior executive cannot function in a knowledge vacuum. How can you take the necessary action to advance your business if you're not aware of what people are thinking or where their real concerns might lie?

Enter the Chief. Or the truth teller. Like a jester in a Shakespearean play (if a little less fun). As a senior exec, you need truth like you need air. Your Chief will understand what's really happening out there and then speak truth to power.

| You need truth like you need air.

They know you don't enjoy bad news, but that you need to hear it. A Chief understands that you should never be surprised. They know what matters and, as importantly, what can be sorted out without your involvement. They know you can't perform at your best unless you're informed. Your Chief protects you from misdirecting your time, or by stopping you from acting based on misunderstandings, misconceptions, and poor information. You need accuracy and honesty to make the right decisions, and your Chief is primed to offer these things.

Ignorance Isn't Bliss (in the C-Suite)

David Dunning's 2011 article in the scholarly journal *Advances in Experimental Psychology* should be a must-read for any senior exec. The title says it all: "On Being Ignorant of One's Own Ignorance." The numbers Dunning's research revealed are startling. In essence, he found that of every C-suite leader asked whether they rank in the top 10% of their field, 90% said "yes."

Imagine asking every child sitting for an exam whether they would get a top grade and having almost all of them predict they'd get an "A." That sort of perception gap can be disastrous for an organization.

My instinct is that the 10% who were more realistic in their self-assessment would work very well with a Chief of Staff. Someone to tell them what they needed to hear. To help them improve as a leader by understanding what wasn't working. The story of "The Emperor's New Clothes" may make children laugh, but it should also be seriously considered by every senior exec.

Compassionate Truth Telling

When I was serving as a Chief, one of my bosses was a great guy we'll call Steve. He became aware that his understanding of what was happening on a particular business initiative didn't match his team's view. He was full of good intentions but some of his recommendations to the team were based on misinformation.

We decided that one of my key roles was to close the gap. He put a lot of trust in me to tell him exactly what he needed to know—and to not wait to be asked. From observing his communication style closely, I recognized that as much as he asked for complete honesty, he reacted best to it being delivered in a certain way.

So, I became his "compassionate truth teller." I told him what he needed to know, even if it was difficult for him to hear. I put our mission above his sensibilities. If he needed to hear it, I told him. That's how I Chiefed and that's how I coach. It's better to be candid than candy-coated. But I was careful to make sure he understood that nothing I said was personal. The best compliment he ever paid me was telling me I was the soul of the team.

It's better to be candid than candy-coated.

Revolutionizing Company Communications

At the start of this chapter, we looked at Trent and his under-performing team. One of his key issues was communication. This meant initiatives were losing traction and slowing down between functions. Team members were interpreting the vision and strategy in different ways.

Truly preventing problems requires everyone involved to understand exactly what's expected. Confusion and productivity are adversaries. Misperceptions hold back teams and businesses. Are you spending too much time cleaning up communication breakdowns? Do your teams seem to fail because they can't relay your key messages?

In some cases, this can be solved by clarifying the messages themselves. But not always. **A good Chief of Staff can identify precisely where the message is getting lost or diluted.**

The fix will depend on the underlying cause. Trent simply had to sit back and get the message across as precisely as possible. In other businesses I've consulted with, I have helped the Chief of Staff create a brand-new communications plan. Some leaders needed to construct a communications matrix, articulating what each member of the team needed to hear and when. Others needed a clearer way of asking questions and resolving misunderstandings.

Either way, your Chief of Staff will help you implement a communication plan that gets the job done.

It could look something like this:

INTERNAL COMMUNICATION PLAN ON HYBRID WORK

Audience	Company-wide, All Employees	Senior Leaders	Front Line Managers
Strategy	Create a sense of inclusion and collaboration in the hybrid work environment, emphasizing the benefits and addressing potential challenges.	Highlight the strategic value of hybrid work in terms of productivity, employee satisfaction, and cost savings.	Provide guidance and support to managers in effectively managing hybrid teams, addressing their concerns, and helping them facilitate team collaboration.
Key Message	Embrace the flexibility and opportunities of hybrid work while maintaining a strong connection with colleagues and the company.	Hybrid work enables us to drive innovation, attract top talent, and achieve our strategic goals.	Hybrid work requires effective leadership to ensure team cohesion, maintain accountability, and support individual growth.
Channel(s)	Town Hall, company-wide email, intranet announcement, and team meetings	Executive briefing session, followed by a memo and Q&A session	Manager training session, manager's toolkit, and follow-up individual consultations
Date	Aug 1	July 15	Aug 15
Materials Due	July 25	July 10	Aug 1
Owner	Internal Comms Team	CEO and HR	HR & Training Development Team

Take the Temperature

I've explained elsewhere how a Chief gets information on how team members are really feeling. That's crucial, but it's only part of the solution. Inspired by business management expert Patrick Lencioni's "5 Behaviors of a Cohesive Team" model, which centers on trust and healthy communication, I am a fan of leadership implementing a quarterly survey focused entirely on these two components.

A quarterly trust and communication survey takes the pulse of the wider team and demonstrates how close people are to understanding and buying into the messages that matter. It's an incredibly efficient way of cleaning the gutters, unblocking potential misunderstandings.

At first, a survey that measures these qualities can be a rather startling eye-opener. In the long term, it's a useful checkup that helps inform a company's leadership and ensures, as ever, that the Chief of Staff is best placed to find and iron out small problems before they become big ones.

Would you shoot an arrow and not look to see if it hit the target? I think not. Measure. Measure. Measure. Improve. Improve. Improve.

The Takeaway

You deserve to step away from the front line. And you owe it to yourself to do your best work in an environment where prevention of problems is a central tenet. That's what a great Chief of Staff can help you do, dealing with things effectively without your involvement, but telling you clearly and honestly what you need to know.

And it's worth repeating again and again that a great Chief really does save you time *while* making you more effective. Whatever will you do with all that extra room to think and create?

Exercise

Grab your notebook again. Write about a problem that took up too much of your time at work, one that should have been dealt with by other staff long before it landed in your lap.

1. What were the consequences of devoting your energy to solving this problem?

2. Try to list everything, large or small, that was impacted by the mishandling of this issue.

3. Jot down how the experience made you feel.

4. What do you wish had gone differently?

CHAPTER 6

Meta Problem 4:
I'm Surrounded by "Yes" People

"The Chief of Staff has to reflect and sometimes complement the strengths of the president he serves."
– William M. Daley, Chief of Staff to Barack Obama

Meet Leilani

Leilani has star quality. A first-generation college student, she fought her way into an Ivy League MBA program. From there, she was hired by a blue-chip company, where she rose quickly through the ranks. She was appointed CEO—their youngest ever. The staff held her in the very highest esteem.

So why did she call me to say she felt adrift? Why did she feel so concerned that she was making poor decisions? Why did she feel that something was wrong, but she couldn't identify it?

I suggested I spend some time observing her at work. And wow, was she good. Maybe too good? She shone so brightly that her team appeared to fawn around her, desperate for her praise. They wanted to bask in her golden shadow. In a staff meeting, everything she proposed was met with overenthusiastic agreement and the diligent scribbling of notes.

When she asked for constructive criticism, the silence was deafening. When she asked for the team's suggestions, heads remained bowed.

Leilani had risen so far, so fast, that she had become a quasi-mythological character in the business. Her presence had people swooning. Her views quickly became gospel. But she was human. And she figured she was probably wrong sometimes. Could her thinking be stagnating? What if one of her big plans was bound to backfire, only she couldn't see it? The situation was risky, and Leilani was desperate to break out of her echo chamber.

This situation wasn't healthy, either. We had work to do.

The Problem with "Yes"

You're almost certainly familiar with the phrase "move with the times." And in the business world, the times have never moved faster than they do today. Keeping yourself moving on that level requires huge amounts of agility and snappy decision-making.

To keep making the best decisions, you need to be challenged. You won't get it right every time, and it's important your team helps you maximize your chances by pushing you, testing the boundaries, and helping you sense what is good and what is going to sink.

> To keep making the best decisions, you need to be challenged.

If nobody offers that challenge (and this may seem unintuitive), the pressure on the leader grows. The team becomes no more than an agency for carrying out orders. Creative tension disappears. The leader is an all-singing, all-dancing, one-person show.

That dynamic will frustrate a leader. It can also cause the CEO to feel burnout and resentment. Real progress is driven by the team, but the leader can see when that progress is waning. Once again, we find an apt parallel in sports . . . The team relies on the star player to come up with the key plays every game, and they enter a comfort zone, waiting for miracles. Meanwhile, the leader is increasingly vulnerable to their own blind spots.

So, here's the irony: Being fabulous doesn't work if it means you keep being told you are fabulous. It only works if your cheerleaders are prepared to question, challenge, and debate you.

What's Driving Your Yes People?

Have you wished your team just told you what they really thought? Fed up with the sycophancy? Do you hear that little voice in your head saying "here we go again" as soon as you've stopped talking and the room falls to babbling praise?

Welcome to the world of celebrity—because that's what's happened to you. Your power and your aura have become a barrier to normality.

Some of your team will fear meeting with your disapproval. Others may be inherently conflict averse. A few may be petrified of losing their job and are working under the misapprehension that you *want* them to keep saying yes.

Within the group, there will be some seriously important points and challenges ready to emerge. There may be someone sitting there ready to raise opposition. But they are waiting for someone else to say something first. No one dares to break the ice.

Creating the Right Atmosphere

You want to lead a team happy to take risks and share ideas. That won't happen until they feel the freedom to do so. You hold the key to that freedom. You are empowered to create an environment in which they feel enough of a sense of psychological safety to raise a hand and join the conversation.

But safety alone isn't enough. They also need to be motivated and to feel accountable for their performance. People in their comfort zone, happy to nod along and enjoy the ride, are not going to push you hard enough.

What you're shooting for is a team so strong you don't know who the boss is.

So, What Do You Do?

Your responsibility is to create an environment where your people are free to work, challenge, think, and dream without fear.

Every member of the team needs to understand not just that you can be challenged, but that you actively encourage it. That you can only perform at your best by being pushed. That you are more likely to make better decisions with their input.

> **Every member of the team needs to understand not just that you can be challenged, but that you actively encourage it.**

You know that you have built this team for a purpose. Time and care went into assembling a world-class team. You have diverse people with different skills who look at the world in different ways. Your role is to nurture, not to silence.

That means:

- Setting clear goals and expectations
- Providing feedback
- Offering rewards and recognition

It means holding every member of your team accountable for themselves and their contribution to the wider group.

JACKSON *before* ALICIA

Jackson is your typical outdoorsy kind of guy. He's also highly intelligent. One day on the trails, he had an idea, and within a decade, he'd leveraged that concept into a hugely successful brand. In fact, you might just have a piece of his company's clothing hanging in your closet. The problem was that Jackson's team was starstruck. So, when it came to critiques of the business or Jackson's choices— concerns a CEO really should hear—the people he worked with were mute. *I may as well be doing the job in a studio before an audience*, he thought. *Applause again, please, for my genius. And meanwhile, I'll figure everything out by myself!*

JACKSON *after* ALICIA

When Alicia joined as Jackson's Chief of Staff, things began to change. She used a variety of methods to cultivate a climate of free expression. One highlight was the weekly team hike, and not just because it got Jackson back out on the trails he loved. It proved to be a time when everyone could help each other over slippery rocks, literally and metaphorically. Before long, they were talking to Jackson with candor and challenging his ideas. And with a diversity of visions and voices, the company went to even higher heights!

Bring on the Chief!

It's rare that I reach this point in the chapter without mentioning the Chief of Staff. But this is a problem that needs to be fully understood before you can truly see the value a great Chief can bring.

Your relationship with your Chief of Staff needs to become the foundation for the way you want relationships to flourish within the team. Your Chief must feel safe to openly share ideas, concerns, and feedback with you. On the flip side, they must never fear negative consequences for speaking up. Your relationship will prosper, and your team will follow.

Creating a psychologically safe relationship with your Chief will energize you, improving your perspective and your decision-making. I know of one Chief of Staff who served a CEO in the telecommunications sector and was renowned for her honest, unpolished reflections. If ever she checked in and wondered whether she had gone too far, her leader would reply, "You are always welcome into my kitchen." His kitchen was where he had his closest and most trusting interactions. It is the beating heart of any home. That was one hell of a compliment. And this is the kind of figurative invitation your Chief needs from you.

My executive clients relish this free exchange of ideas. I coach them to communicate in the most transparent ways. Imagine sharing integrity and goals with your ally and adviser. Reaching those goals is easiest when no holds are barred.

Your Chief Becomes the Conduit to Your Team

Sound good? Well, the relationship between you and your Chief is just the start. Among their most important responsibilities is helping coach your team on how to get the best out of you. Your Chief can get them to a place where they will challenge and provoke, blue-sky and imagine.

In the first instance, your team may feel more comfortable doing this with your Chief. Then your Chief can become a gatekeeper—suggesting which ideas they take to you directly. They can guide and cajole, improving the quality of internal dialogue and stressing the importance of psychological safety.

Your Chief will have time to navigate the politics of the workplace; they will instinctively understand where the best ideas and challenges are being stymied. A great Chief will unlock, empower, and keep engagement strong. How could that change your world?

Your Chief Can Build Your Culture

A Chief acts as your eyes and ears in and around the business. A great Chief takes things further and helps create a culture supporting honest expression.

Forbes has attempted to list the qualities required in such a culture. It's a long and detailed list, so let me paraphrase:

What characterizes a healthy and robust organizational culture? Authenticity and empathy. Asking tough questions and then listening hard. Adopting a positive service mindset with colleagues while being prepared to challenge each other constructively. Including connecting while staying neutral in negative situations.

Dr. Jamie Shapiro, CEO leadership coach, suggests that a Chief of Staff can encourage a culture in which empathy, authenticity, and vitality become habitual. A CoS can help to reinforce team expectations and behavior that foster a cohesive team culture and, when the culture is right, the hard miles become easier, and your goals become realities.

> **A CoS can encourage a culture in which empathy, authenticity, and vitality become habitual.**
> **—Dr. Jamie Shapiro**

Additionally, her powerful new research links factors that create psychological safety to vitality in leadership—both foundational in creating healthy cultures. For more on this topic, I highly recommend Dr. Jamie Shapiro's work, which you can find at www.connectedec.com.

The Truth Will Set You Free

Have there been times when you felt like Leilani? Well, here's an idea. Don't be seduced by "yes." Use your Chief: first as a sounding board, then as an example for the relationships you are looking to develop, and finally as someone who can create a culture of honesty, safety, and motivation.

Encourage Your Chief to Use the Johari Window

We all have blindspots, and to be a more effective leader, your Chief can help you identify yours through a practical tool called the Johari Window. Developed in 1955 by psychologists Joseph Luft and Harrington Ingham, the framework is a simple and elegant way of representing and understanding interpersonal relationships.

	Known to Self	**Unknown to Self**
Known to Others	Open area	**Blind area**
Unknown to Others	**Hidden area**	Unknown area

In my experience, the Johari window can quickly shed light on the attitudes and misunderstandings potentially holding you back right now. Oftentimes, how we see ourselves may differ from how others perceive us. My clients love this tool because it directly fosters more authenticity and awareness in their relationships. You can find a number of tutorials online with details on how to use it.

And How About Leilani?

Well, now, she's just great! We hired her a smart, high-energy Chief of Staff. The Chief was assigned the task of building an environment that welcomed a true diversity of perspectives.

Within weeks, Leilani was being challenged. Her ideas were sharpened. And she was receiving the new thinking and perspectives she had so desperately wanted. She celebrated the contributions of others who now understood exactly what she wanted from them. Her depression lifted.

While I was proofreading this book, Leilani emailed me. "Work," she reported, "is actually becoming fun, and I mean fun for everyone." Turns out that when the team is empowered to say "no," the leader—and indeed the whole company—move forward with a resounding "yes!"

Exercise

Take a few minutes to write about the most fruitful disagreement you can remember having at work.

1. What was at issue?

2. How did you feel?

3. And what, if any, changes resulted from the conversation?

CHAPTER 7

How to Hire and Launch Your New Chief of Staff

"Bruce has been an invaluable partner and adviser, playing a key role in driving the company's strategic direction and growth."
— Marilyn Hewson, CEO of Lockheed Martin, on Chief of Staff Bruce Tanner

I f you only read one chapter, read this one. Yes, this one's crucial. Because you don't just need *a* Chief of Staff. You need the right Chief of Staff for *you*.

The Chief of Staff is an elevated role. Treat it that way. One of my CEOs shared that of the many Chiefs he's had in his career, the vast majority of them went on to become CEOs or C-suite leaders later in their careers. This is no doubt a developmental role for a future leader of the company. It gives others exposure to them and gives them exposure to the broader domain of business. It's truly the best development job you can give anyone.

You want a Chief because you don't have time to focus on what matters. But making this decision requires time. So, invest that time, because getting it right will change everything in terms of your performance and ability to drive impact.

Let's Get Started: Essential Criteria

No matter what your strengths, weaknesses, hopes, or dreams are, there's an inventory of "must have" qualities for every Chief. I'd suggest that every candidate should tick most of these boxes:

- ☐ MBA or Chief of Staff experience
- ☐ Experienced at planning and leading strategic initiatives
- ☐ Strong background in cross-functional and interdepartmental engagement
- ☐ Strong business and financial acumen, as well as a strong understanding of a profit and loss statement
- ☐ Comfortable with ambiguity and bias towards action
- ☐ Open to a wide variety of perspectives, including ones that run counter to their own
- ☐ Extremely versatile, dedicated to efficient productivity
- ☐ Skilled at driving alignment (and driving harmony is a real plus!)
- ☐ Aptitude for being highly influential between functions
- ☐ 6+ years of professional experience in a leadership role—optimal if it's consulting or financial
- ☐ Commitment to quality and excellence in *everything*!

A Chief Can See What You Can't See

They are your back door into the organization. They are your eyes and ears. They amplify what you need to do in your role to be most impactful.

They Are Respected, Not Feared

What does this mean? They are trusted by their colleagues. They are friendly and approachable with a firm aura of accountability and commitment. They are collaborative, effective, empathetic, and driven by results. They enable a productive culture.

Now Let's Personalize This to Your Needs

If that's what every Chief needs to offer at the core, what do you need in addition?

Here are some prompts to map your specific needs against a standard job description. It's time to grab that notebook again:

1. What does your organization or mission need most from you right now?

2. What impact are you looking to drive for your shareholders, your customers, and your employees?

3. Where do you urgently need help? Just writing this bucket list will leave you feeling more positive!

4. Where do you sense you would benefit from further strategic support?

5. Where does your leadership team think you could benefit from more support?

6. Pinpoint the qualities you would relish in a Chief of Staff. Envision your dream Chief.

That description should be starting to take shape already. You need someone in your corner who is going to offer everything you need to achieve your potential. Someone who "gets" the mission and who "gets" you. A Chief who is strong where you are relatively weak. A Chief who is knowledgeable and passionate about the job with ground-level business experience. Someone able to build trust and form a strong bond with you now and into the future. What particulars have you added to envision the Chief who is exactly the right match for *you*?

Engage Your Leadership Team

You will instinctively know what you "want" in your Chief of Staff. And your colleagues will often have a better idea of what you actually "need." This is such an important step.

Take Joanne, a C-suite executive at a major tech company. She knew she needed a Chief and she asked me to help her find the right candidate. Before we started our search, we ran a quick survey to see what qualities her team felt she'd benefit from in a Chief. Their list and hers looked very different!

Simply by asking the right questions of her team, Joanne benefited from a much clearer understanding of how her needs were perceived. The team's understanding of Joanne filled the gaps in the vision she held in her mind, enabling her to hire the Chief who was truly the right match. And the team welcomed the new Chief with open arms, as they felt integral to the process and the relationship that followed.

Need a Little More Guidance?

You've thought through what you want. You've gotten input on what you may not have realized you need. Those steps are crucial. And in defining your optimal Chief, it's important to make this process as objective as possible. The following matrix can help determine many of the qualities required from a hire at various levels through a business. It may help you tighten that job spec yet further. The aim is that you will know precisely what you need before you invite candidates to apply.

Who Has Your Back?

Role Level	Level 1	Level 2
Leveling Equivalent	Assoc.	Sr. Assoc./ Jr. Mgr
Alternate Titles	Founder's Associate, Generalist, Business Operations Associate	Generalist, Business Operations Manager
Relationship to Principal	Operates with little independence Explicit direction from Principal	Operates with some independence Regular check-ins with Principal
Primary Directive	Optimize Principal's time; body man, accompanies Principal to key meetings	Expand Principal's time—takes projects off their plate
Scope of Role	Execute on small project or tasks	Manage small projects
Decision Making Capabilities	Not involved in strategic decisions	Implement strategic decisions
Influence/ Leadership	Strong relationships, but low influence across organization	Horsepower, manage by influence primarily with Principal
Demonstrated Skills	Attention to detail, strong work ethic, and super organizer	Strong operational and strategy experience, ability to drive business insights and operational improvement
Responsibility Examples	Ensure the executive team is working on the most important items for the company	Create investor updates, pitch decks, speeches, conference submissions, and presentations on behalf of the CEO
Direct Reports	None	None
Exit Path	Entry-level product or operations roles; HR/ People Ops	Founder; Business Operations or Strategy roles, Business School

Level 3	Level 4	Level 5
Mgr/ Sr. Mgr	Director	Executive
Founder's Associate, Generalist, Business Operations Manager	Director, Office of the CEO, Head of Business Operations	CAO, COO, VP Strategy
Operates with some independence Regular/occasional check-ins with Principal	Operates mostly independently Little operational supervision, but occasional check-ins with Principal	Operates independently No operational supervision
Expand Principal's time and influence on cross-functional projects	Takes Principal's key priorities and selects, scopes, and completes projects to fulfill them	Has their own priorities related to overall company objectives
Own assigned projects end-to-end	Scope, own, and manage projects to completion. Some self-directed work.	Strategic Owner
Input on strategic decisions	Key influencer on strategic decisions	Key owner & decision maker
Thought partner to Principal; manage by influence across Senior Leadership Team	Key thought partner across leadership team; manage by influence across organization	Direct management, strategy leadership
Strong project management coordination & reporting experience	Experience leading a team & interacting with senior stakeholders on cross-functional projects	Expert at stakeholder management and Senior Leadership Team facilitating & influencing
Initiate and guide the OKR process across the company	Run special projects that are urgent and important	Serve as a proxy for the CEO by attending meetings in place of the CEO and making decisions on the CEO's behalf
Maybe an EA	Office of the CEO	Department
Founder, General Manager, Sr. Associate in Venture Capital	Senior Leadership; General Manager, VP roles (Operations, Strategy, Corp Dev. People, etc.)	Other exec roles, leading smaller organizations

Establish Your Interview Squad

You're not going to go through the hiring process alone. You want to hire someone you can trust and get along with, as you will spend a significant amount of time together. But this isn't just about resonating with the candidate. It's about bringing in a valued resource to the very heart of the team. That means your direct reports need to feel a sense of ownership in the hire. You've asked them to delineate the kind of Chief they think you need. Now, involve them further by gathering an interview squad of your direct reports and key team members, headed by your HR leader.

Run the Search (And Look in Unexpected Places!)

Ideally, the HR leader should start the search internally over a week to ten days. No more than that. It's ideal to find a candidate who is already part of the company. That individual will be familiar with the culture, leaders, and overall mission of your business. This will shorten transition time so they can hit the ground running.

I believe in hunting for your Chief in unexpected places. Look at the strategy team for broad thinkers. Look for the quarterback who led the last high-profile company initiative. Scan for someone the team finds invaluable but who never asks for recognition.

If no qualified candidates surface, then it's time to expand the search externally. Ask a trusted set of leaders in your network for referrals (and make yourself available to do the same for them in the future). While this particular outreach may seem an obvious request, I am shocked to see how often it's overlooked.

Have your HR leader or equivalent screen the candidates and do the initial interviewing. Require that candidates submit a work product as part of the application process to qualify for the position. Or pose a question/problem and ask them how they'd approach solving it. Bottom line: only the best two or three candidates make it through the process to meet with you.

Notice the movement toward resourcing yourself with outside support? And you don't even have your Chief hired yet!

Conduct the Interview

A poor interview can leave you blind to a person's strengths—or even worse, to their weaknesses. Preparation is vital. Here's an interview matrix I designed (with input from many other excellent Chiefs of Staff) and have used with consistent success. It covers the most important questions that will tease out what you want to know and what you want to see in your candidates:

CHIEF OF STAFF INTERVIEW QUESTIONS

Select the questions most relevant to your candidate and the opportunity

General | You | The Role

- Tell me about yourself—professionally and personally.
- What excites you most about this role?
- What aspect do you anticipate being the most challenging?
- What or who motivates and inspires you? And why?
- What is it like to experience you at your BEST— and WORST?

Attributes

- Relationship development, building trust, and loyalty are key in this role. Talk about what these mean to you in relation to your working style. How would you go about establishing relationships and trust with (hiring leader) DRs?
- Oftentimes, growth comes through challenging the status quo—talk about a time when you did this and how it benefited your work or an outcome.
- The ability to absorb, seek out, and process high volumes of new information is normal in this role at "company." What does continuous learning look like for you? (Look for internal and external in their answer.)

Process

- This role will regularly put you in unanticipated situations where you are dealing with competing priorities under pressure. What is your default style/behavioral tendencies when under stress and how do you manage them?

- Talk about your process of prioritizing, establishing direction, and delegation.

- How do you manage conflict, especially with strong personalities?

- Tell me about a time when you had to analyze information and make a recommendation. What's your approach? How did it turn out?

- Being resourceful is essential in this role—with little to no direction. Talk about being resourceful and how you'd leverage it in this role. Please provide examples.

- What would your approach to the first 60 days look like?

- When you face an unanticipated or less-than-favorable outcome, it's important to be resilient (learn and move forward). Talk about how resilient you are and provide examples.

Evaluate the Intangibles

As is true for all of us, you are absolutely unique. Your leadership style, your strengths, and your weaknesses are nuanced. There will be situations that simply call for a helpful word from your Chief. In other areas, your Chief will ensure you are getting it right. And sometimes, you'll need to hear the hard truth in a way that makes sense and motivates you. They need to understand not only what you do but how you feel. This is a "relationship" in the truest sense of the word.

So, the interview needs to hone in on personality, character, and chemistry. You need to test soft skills as well as qualifications and hard facts, asking questions like "What would you do if you were faced with X?" and "When have you experienced Y, and how did you respond?"

This will reveal different skills and aptitudes than a resume can reflect. Posing hypotheticals will enable you to make a more informed call on these crucial clusters of qualities:

1. Vision; resourcefulness

2. Diplomacy; humility; sincerity; self-awareness; emotional intelligence

3. Clear and relevant communication

4. Kindness and the capacity to learn quickly

5. The ability to operate well both as an individual contributor and as a team member

6. Comfort with conflict

7. Driving influence and alignment

Chemistry Is Key

You're asking all the right questions to reveal a potential Chief's professional qualities, the skills and more subtle capabilities they would bring to the position. Your interview isn't complete, however, unless you get a clear read on the chemistry between you. Chemistry is important in any relationship and its essential with your Chief of Staff. We flourish when we work with someone who provides the yin to our yang. How do you create that? And how do you assess it, particularly in an interview?

Where chemistry exists, you will find it easy to chat. There will be times when you are able to finish each other's sentences. You won't feel that sense of irritation that can seep into conversations for no obvious reason. You'll enjoy the prospect of meeting again and of spending more time together. It's hard to define but easy to identify when it happens.

Bottom line: Be uncompromising at selecting talent for this role. It's one of the—if not *the*—most important hires you'll ever make.

So Now You've Found the Chief of Your Dreams!

The prep, team effort, networking, HR blast, and highly refined interview process have finally led to what you dreamed would happen. You have identified the candidate you want as your new Chief of Staff, and they're going to change your life.

Congratulations! But don't sit back yet. Make sure your offer is competitive. While compensation for a Chief of Staff varies, the most common components are:

Base Salary: This can vary widely based on the factors including industry, company size, geographic location, level of experience, and the specific responsibilities and scope of the role. Generally, base salary ranges from mid- to high six-figure salaries.

Bonuses: Chiefs are typically eligible for performance-based bonuses or incentives tied to the achievement of the company goals or targets.

Stock Options or Equity Grants: In some cases, Chiefs may receive stock options or equity grants as part of their compensation package. This is typical with founder CEOs and startups. This allows your Chief to have a stake in the company's success and can provide a potentially substantial financial reward if the organization performs well.

Benefits and Perks: Chiefs typically receive a comprehensive benefits package, including health insurance, retirement plans, and paid time off. They might also have access to executive perks such as expense accounts, company cars, or executive retreats.

Bottom line, they need to value you as much as you value them, so be sure to indicate your seriousness from the start. Remember, your investment in your Chief is likely to pay off beyond measure.

And if you've read this far, you know that this relationship is a precious one, and it should be handled accordingly. That means, of course, that you can't just sit back and expect your new Chief to take the reins the moment they arrive, to know all you need and do everything with ease. Care needs to be taken to set up your new Chief for success. So now, I'm going to walk you through a series of steps I've found to be critical in this process.

Establish the Reporting Structure

The Chief should report directly to the CEO, alongside the SVPs and those in other leadership roles. Make sure all parties are aware of this.

For a visual example, this diagram shows you a reporting structure adapted from the common corporate leadership design.

ORGANIZATIONAL CHART

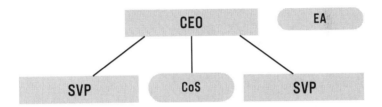

Communicate the Chief's Role to Your Team

Don't leave your direct reports in the dark. They must be part of this new relationship. Your job is to explain what's changing, thoughtfully and with consideration for their existing patterns of workflow and responsibility.

Your wider team likewise needs to know who this new person is and why they are there. Introducing the Chief's position with care will go a long way toward establishing trust and openness among the team. It can also create an opportunity to be open about the shortfalls in your leadership that will be directly addressed by the appointment. This is an important juncture, and it's a chance to build toward increased positivity moving forward.

You might want to explain your Chief's role with language like this:

"Tina has joined our leadership team to help us perform better, particularly in terms of my relationship with all of you. She will be responsible for supporting my mission to make the organization run smoothly and efficiently. She will serve as my partner, communicating my expectations around your responsibilities and roles. I ask you to speak as openly and honestly to her as you would to me, and to use her as a conduit for messages you would like me to receive when you can't reach me directly."

Starting to Work Together

1. Take Time to Know Each Other Better

Your bond will benefit both you and your business. So, make time for a coffee. Go out for lunch. Often. Get to know each other. Understand each other's personal lives. Talk through interesting and complicated aspects of your approaches to work and life. This will help you avoid awkward issues or misunderstandings. Your relationship to your Chief demands a substantive investment from you.

| **Your bond will benefit both you and your business.**

And especially in the beginning, you're the one setting the tone. Show up with your best self, your most honest and open heart, and your vulnerability—your humanness—to pave the way for a connection that will ultimately benefit you both. A few key questions to ask each other as you start working together:

How do you like to consume information (email, voicemail, live meetings, etc.)? How do you want us to communicate (text, one-on-one, voicemail, etc.)? What would you like our rhythm of connection to be for how/when we'll meet (daily, weekly or other)?

Establish the boundaries of confidentiality. They will be privy to information and critical decisions that will help shape the company. Trust is essential. Explain the importance of this commitment and that if they break confidence, they are out. It's an honor and privilege to serve in this role. Treat it that way.

2. Ignite Your New Chief with the Right Work

Your Chief will become your greatest asset. Empower them. They will save you time and transform your world. But they won't do it on their first morning on the job.

Don't expect miracles. A personal chef needs to understand your lifestyle and dietary nuances. A personal trainer needs to get to know your physicality. Similarly, a Chief of Staff needs to grow into the role, exploring the best ways to serve you and support the business.

One of the greatest leaders I have ever worked with had each of his new Chiefs of Staff read these two books as they started the role: *Say It with Charts: The Executive's Guide to Visual Communication* by Gene Zelanzy and *The Pyramid Principle* by Barbara Minto. He believed that those books were foundational to success and to the Chief role specifically. He was right. Each of his Chiefs *killed* it in the role when working with him. The key messages in both books helped him to establish his values, properly communicate, and avoid pitfalls.

Once you've communicated your baselines and boundaries, I recommend starting with a single project that requires time and consideration, along with a handful of diverse and easily achievable tasks. This will save you time while you're putting your Chief in contact with various departments, challenges, and key players.

Let your Chief get a quick sense of who's who, what's working, what's not, and how the structure operates. This may use up some of your time in the short term, but the benefits will be exponential.

Establish how you want things to work. Ensure your Chief doesn't overuse your name or carry it with them in order to get things done or to make requests of the leaders. Your Chief should avoid saying things like "John asked for this . . ." and "John wants this by . . ." Carrying your name with a request not only dilutes the Chief's leadership, but it will also dilute their ability to maintain the strength of a strategic ask of the team/business on their own. This is important at the start and sets the stage for the Chief's entire term.

3. Measure Success

You may already have a sense of how this new dynamic should go. You'll sleep better, arrive at work in a better frame of mind, and be able to focus your attention on what really matters. Which is great. But what about your Chief? They will need very clear targets from the start. Define and be transparent about how you'll measure the success of your Chief of Staff.

Measurements might be: a more engaged employee base, increase in productivity, speed in launching initiatives, you never feeling rushed, you always being prepared . . . get the picture?

With those measures agreed upon, you also need regular check-ins to understand how your Chief is feeling. You don't want to create a situation where they end up as stressed and overloaded as you were before you hired them!

That means formal monthly check-ins where you ask how "it" is going, how "we" are doing, and, most importantly, how "you" are doing.

You need to make it clear that you can adjust things to make your Chief's life better. This is a two-way relationship. Invest in them, nurture them, and coach them. If things are going "okay," but your goals exceed what your Chief is achieving, a coaching program with an outside expert may well take your relationship up a notch. I offer a coaching engagement called RAMP (Relationship Amplified) where I work with the leader and the Chief in the same engagement. The agenda is bespoke, and all designed around what is most important to *you* and your mission. In a nutshell, I set you both up for success.

If You Get It Right

If all goes well, with the right person and management of the relationship, you will experience your Chief coming in every day:

- Operating with confidence
- Feeling inspired and directed by you

- Receiving support and respect from your leadership team

- Assuming command and control with ease

- Challenging your thinking and offering new perspectives

- Delegating comfortably

- Providing you with trusted advice and guidance

- Driving strong results and impact

If it's working well and the relationship appears to be working perfectly, push harder. Ask your Chief what more you can do. What dreams can you reach for? What is it possible for you to create together?

And There's More

If you have hired the right person, you are one step away from success. And that step is contingent on how you manage them. You will have gotten this wrong if your Chief becomes a note-taker in meetings or a "cascader" of actions. They should be focused on higher-level challenges. Your directors are executives and are responsible for walking away from a meeting with their own action items.

Don't give your Chief "work" or to-do lists. Give them problems that tap into their creative genius, delve into their strategic mind-set, and will add measurable value to your world when solved.

If, after all that, you feel that you have time to focus on the real priorities and start to execute them, then you've gotten it right.

What to Do if All Goes Wrong

Unfortunately, all the world's planning and preparation can't protect you from the possibility that you and your new Chief of Staff aren't a match after all.

If you realize that the problem isn't a case of early misunderstandings or hiccups, but a genuine lack of chemistry, don't hold on for too long. Respectfully and directly share your concerns, and if you don't think the bleeding can be stemmed (or you don't want to take the time to stem it), offer to help them look for a role elsewhere in the business. This is not a "failure." You just need a better match. Great people don't always make a great marriage.

The good news? The work you have done and plans you have made will make a second appointment much easier. The transition should be smoother, and you will have learned from what did and didn't work.

And if your relationship with your Chief isn't functioning well and is still worth investing in, I've dedicated the next chapter to all the ways you can reset and reboot for success.

JERRY *before* ANTON

A senior executive for an automotive giant, Jerry wore a mask of absolute confidence. Behind it, he was beyond overwhelmed and deeply afraid he would drop the ball. He couldn't keep on top of his major initiatives because he was overloaded with smaller projects, he didn't trust his reports enough to delegate sufficiently, and he had no time to figure out how to manage his time. But Jerry was no dummy. He recognized he needed support. Periodically, his heart thumping, he paused to imagine a life that involved someone who had his back. Thankfully, someone gave him my number.

JERRY *after* ANTON

With a bit of coaching, Jerry slowed down. Understanding how important the process was, he took time with every phase of the search. Within a month, he had hired an ideal candidate, Anton, an organized powerhouse of a veteran Chief whose chemistry with Jerry was palpable. And Jerry invested his energy in establishing that relationship. Their morning check-ins and weekly lunches involved hard conversations, but those talks were built on trust. And peppered with laughter. Six years later, Jerry's company's revenue quadrupled. And Jerry reported he loves his time off. "Reading for pleasure, candlelit date nights with my wife, family dinners where the kids know I'm present enough to listen—actually listen. Thank you, Anton."

Exercise

Once you've secured the Chief of Staff you need, have a session to challenge each other on what dreaming bigger might look like for both of you—and for the extended team. What could you gain by dreaming bigger? Exploring your visions for the future is a great way to build your interpersonal connection while you work together to elevate and transform your business. Plus, it's fun, and (duh) having fun with each other strengthens your relationship. Ask each other some questions like these:

1. What is one thing we can do better that would be a game changer for us and our team?

2. Then what?

3. How can we expand our market reach and tap into new customer segments?

4. What innovative strategies can we implement to stay ahead of our competitors?

5. How can we foster a culture of creativity and innovation within the team?

6. What are some potential partnerships or collaborations that can drive significant growth for our business?

7. How can we leverage emerging technologies to enhance our products or services?

8. In what ways can we improve our customer experience and build long-lasting relationships?

9. What steps can we take to attract and retain top talent in the industry?

10. What are some unconventional or out-of-the-box ideas that can disrupt our industry and lead to exponential growth?

11. How can we leverage data and analytics to make informed business decisions and drive continuous improvement?

CHAPTER 8

I'm Trying and Trying, but It's Not Working Out!

"Leadership is not about being in charge,
it's about taking care of those in your charge."
– Simon Sinek

Tim and Sarah—a Relationship in Freefall

My client Tim called me to say he was really struggling. Tim is a strong CEO, who had appointed a Chief of Staff to relieve him of the building pressure he felt in his new role. Sarah had seemed like a great match when he hired her. Her experience was substantial; she "understood" the business and seemed to have all the tools required. He felt great about it and was excited to get to work together. What could go wrong?

But as the days and weeks rolled by, it just wasn't working for him, even though he did not want to admit it, because the team had put so much effort into recruiting Sarah and onboarding her. But Tim needed a real, proactive partner. He wanted someone out there in the business, sniffing out problems and finding answers before they reached his desk. And that wasn't happening.

Sarah preferred to be managed. She liked to be given a to-do list. To implement instructions. To assist rather than share the burden of leadership. These traits were not apparent in Tim's interview of Sarah (see interview questions in the previous chapter).

Tim—who is not a fan of confrontation—started to react badly, becoming increasingly irritated. Sarah sensed his frustration and began to feel intimidated. They were both good people, with amazing skills and proven track records. But they just weren't jamming. And the team around them could feel the tense energy in the office. The trust between Tim and Sarah was clearly eroding. When Tim called me, he described their relationship as "spiraling." And once you are in a spiral, it's pretty hard to tell which way is up. He asked me to help him think about a way to better the relationship. He wanted it to work, and he was willing to do his part. I welcomed the opportunity to jump in.

Saving Tim and Sarah

I met with each of them separately, asked a lot of questions, and studied their partnership. I helped each of them identify the areas that were working, before running through those that weren't. It became clear that the problem wasn't one of lack of chemistry, but of understanding *and* communication.

As a result of this work, Tim realized that by taking a helicopter view of the team and his business, he could identify a whole host of responsibilities to delegate to Sarah and give her full ownership. Tim knew that once he'd handed a job to her, he'd never have to worry about it again. He also started giving Sarah problems to run with and encouraged her to find the solutions on her own. This stretched her past her comfort zone of implementation and tapped into her ability to get creative and think strategically. His support and praise built her confidence, and soon Sarah was performing in just the way Tim had hoped she would. Sarah reveled in the new approach, allowing Tim to spend increased time with his team and become more of a hands-on leader.

Within three months, they were working together to create magic. The positive energy and impact rippled through the leadership team. Same people. Different dynamic. Complete recalibration. Bingo!

How Can You Correct Your Leader / Chief Relationship?

You and your Chief may have the occasional dip. What relationship doesn't? But a bad patch doesn't necessarily need to lead straight to a breakup. You can find your way back with a few simple steps:

- *Step one* is honesty. It's daunting to be up-front with someone you work with closely every day. But unless you both communicate truthfully about the rough stuff in your working relationship, you won't find a way to resolve it.

- *Step two* is positivity. Without it, you're both likely to feel shaky, angry, hurt, and distrustful. Positivity greases the wheels. And all it comes down to is going into that conversation wanting to find a solution.

- *Step three* is commitment. From both of you, to changing your dynamic for the better. This one is simple, and it makes all the difference.

And so begins the handshake meeting, where all expectations are shared and clearly defined. There's you, there's your Chief, and then there's the relationship.

Do We Have a Problem Here?

Once you have both agreed you want to make the effort, you can embark on the process of relationship correction. Take some time to align your visions of what success looks and feels like—in most cases, the outcome is a stronger, healthier relationship. Particularly when you follow a tried and trusted route to get there. Here are some questions, reflections, techniques, and suggestions that consistently work for my clients.

Begin by asking yourself these questions that link to the Chief's impact. Are they:

- Successfully communicating your vision and goals to the rest of the team?

- Creating clarity on your behalf?

- Contributing to progress?

- Saving you time and enabling you to focus?

- Delegating with precision and responsibility?

Your questions should, of course, be personalized to reflect your Chief's specific job description. In the short term, the analysis will clarify how much of a problem you have.

The assessment on the next page is a great tool for helping you understand the effectiveness of your Chief of Staff.

How Effective Is Your Chief of Staff

	Struggling	Striving
Rating	**1 2 3**	**4 5 6**
Gatekeeper	Not controlling access to you at all.	Controlling access, but boundaries aren't clear.
Thought Partner	They struggle to identify feedback to give to you.	They are selective with what they share with you.
Problem Seeker & Solver	They are completely reactive.	They're comfortable solving problems when they are well-defined or assigned to them.
Bridge Builder	They work in silos and struggle to manage differing opinions in group settings.	They step up when needed, but often take a backseat in group settings.
Alignment Driver	They struggle to connect daily tasks and efforts to the overall company strategy.	They understand purpose and strategy but don't encourage collaboration over individual contribution.
Powerful Communicator	They avoid speaking up in meetings or sharing their true opinion.	They present their thoughts and ideas when they have time to prepare a presentation or communication plan.
Confidant	They take in confidential information and can't contain it.	They have a basic understanding of what information needs to be kept confidential.

Conventional Success	Extraordinary Success	Now	6 mo
7 8 9	**10 11 12**	**0–12**	**0–12**
They powerfully make decisions around who, how, when someone speaks to you.	People know and trust them to show up and speak confidently on behalf of you.		
They anticipate your needs and drive meaningful conversation to enable decision making.	They're an extension of you and you depend on them to challenge your thinking.		
They know the details of the business to anticipate and avert problems. They're proactive in minimizing risk and taking action.	They never drop the ball. You depend on them to perform powerfully during change and uncertainty.		
They can synthesize multiple points of view and align on direction in an impartial and professional way.	They are able to delegate with ease, mediate conflict, and drive influence between silos.		
They communicate goals and strategy to team members but struggle driving commitment across the team.	They play a key role in communicating and implementing the company's strategy on every level.		
Strong ability to communicate with others effectively in meetings, presentations, and hallway conversations. Excellent active listener.	They have the temperament and tools to facilitate meaningful dialogue and drive progress on initiatives.		
They have a deep understanding of the business and manage sensitive information in confidence and with discretion.	You trust them with any confidential information.		

I recommend you leverage this assessment each quarter: once by you and once by your Chief. Meet to see if you are both aligned in your evaluation of the Chief's performance and to check on progress. In the short term, the analysis can also be highly effective at clarifying problems when the relationship is rocky. This assessment is also a great tool to reflect upon when you're doing your Chief's performance review at the end of the year.

When There's Work to be Done

If, indeed, you feel there's work to do, I suggest you don't start by pointing fingers (see Step 2: Positivity, a few pages prior to here). We all know where that can lead. Instead, consider—and I mean really look at—your own contributions to the tensions between you. Leading in general is no cakewalk, and establishing a vibrant relationship with an intimate aide may be an entirely new kind of walk for you. And again, you are by no means alone in this sort of struggle. Here are some of the most common mistakes I watch CEOs make with their Chiefs.

1. Lack of Clarity, Specificity, and Direction

You haven't been clear enough. Your Chief thinks that all is well—but you don't. This is happening largely because you and your Chief don't share the same "wish list" for their responsibilities.

The root cause of this disconnect is likely a misalignment of expectations and responsibilities. As the leader, you have a specific set of desired outcomes or goals for your Chief's performance, which may not align with what your Chief believes their responsibilities entail. This can create ambiguity and a lack of clarity regarding the Chief's role and what is expected of them.

By discussing your respective "wish lists," you and your Chief can clarify your individual perspectives and reach a shared understanding of what should be prioritized and accomplished. This will bridge the gap in expectations and bring about greater clarity and direction in your working relationship.

Open and transparent communication about both of your expectations can help establish a common ground, fostering a better understanding of each other's roles and responsibilities.

Sometimes this simple realignment of your expectations is all you need.

2. Absence of Feedback

You haven't given your Chief any clue that you're disappointed. You smile stoically, hiding your disappointment when they ask how you are, so they happily keep doing what they're doing. Feedback is crucial to any relationship. You can be honest and constructive. The right Chief will understand and adapt as soon as they become aware there's an issue. If you need help offering feedback to a Chief, or any other leader on your team for that matter, I recommend the book *Thanks for the Feedback*, a great resource by Douglas Stone and Sheila Heen.

| Feedback is crucial to any relationship.

3. Losing Sight of Priorities

You started with a long list of things you needed done, and then you sat back and left your Chief to them. Your Chief created a structure around the list and interpreted their priorities. They feel they're plowing through their work. You feel that they aren't focusing on what matters. The result: disappointment for you both.

The cure: a daily huddle between you both. Have a brief morning meeting to touch base on the day's content, tee up key decisions that need to be made, discuss issues that need to be addressed, and confirm priorities, tasks, and timeframes.

The result: progress! This regular check-in enables you to "Trust but verify," nurturing your relationship while ensuring certainty.

4. The Cardinal Sin of Micromanaging

You hired a Chief to free up your time and energy. But you can't stop yourself from jumping in and micromanaging their tasks. You constantly ask about progress and use spare moments to complete action items on their to-do list.

This is, quite simply, the worst thing you can do as a leader. Take a moment to step into your Chief's shoes. Micromanagement displays a lack of trust, undermines their confidence, and makes redundant your entire quest for a Chief. Embrace their autonomy! Let them work freely, safe in the knowledge that you have their back, and they will have yours.

The Simple Solution

Life isn't always quite so simple. It may be that you can't quite put your finger on the reason the relationship is faltering. Do you feel frustrated but can't explain why?

That's normal. I'd break the spell by enlisting an executive coach or accountability partner who is entirely objective and trained in improvement strategies. Coaches are experts in spotting causes, ironing out misunderstandings, managing blind spots, and aligning expectations. Bring your confusion and distress to the table. A skilled outside specialist will know how to serve up positive change.

In Celebration of Calibration

I want to emphasize a crucial point: All partnerships, professional and social, have challenges. There will always be bumps in the road. It's how we meet these challenges that matters. And that starts by trying to do so in a positive, open, and magnanimous way.

This Really Happened

Imagine a gritty TV drama. Two of the key characters are under pressure. They meet in a cavernous, dark, underground parking garage. Their conversation quickly becomes heated. The temperature rises to a boil before anyone can stop it.

Well, that was Trina. A Chief of Staff with her leader. They had been preparing for an intense operations review with the senior team. Asks were flying at them from every direction. There were too many cooks, creating a lack of clarity. She felt torn between serving her leader and managing others' expectations of him. That scene in the parking lot happened as they both reached the tipping point. It was intense and pretty unforgettable.

Was it time for Trina to look for a new job? Quite the opposite. They departed separately, collected their thoughts, smoothed things out, and made a new plan. They reentered execution mode feeling reinvigorated. Their relationship became richer. To this day, they are both grateful it happened, and even more grateful they were both resilient enough to turn the page and move on afterward.

The lesson: just say it! Don't let a relationship die through lack of communication.

Trust Me—Try to Work It Out

If your relationship with your Chief ever falters, I hope this chapter will help you get that derailed partnership back on track. Disagreements will happen, and they can be healthy—even ultimately transformative—for both of you if handled the right way.

The unique bond between a leader and their Chief relies on candor. There's no room for playing games or sulking. The key is clear communication. Sometimes, you will have to say things the other person may not want to hear. Sometimes, when you're on the listening end, you will need to dig deep into the emotional resources that sustain you, understanding that the vast majority of the time, criticism is constructive and not personal. Check out The Four Agreements by don Miguel Ruiz. He dives into this principle, and once you grasp it, it's life-changing.

Be honest. Be clear. Find a way. Building on the foundation you've lain will result in a much healthier relationship than simply finding the first excuse to rehire and starting the process all over again.

One of my leaders shared with me that feedback is almost always given with good intent. It's given because the person is brave enough to tell you the truth, believes in you, and wants you to do better. It's a gift. That concept shifted me right then and there, and I'll never forget it. It holds true in my life, and I believe it will for you as well.

To quote the great Paul McCartney: "Think of what I'm saying. We can work it out and get it straight or say good night."

KANAE *before* SAM

Sportswear merchandising CEO Kanae was searching for a Chief of Staff to help her streamline her overwhelming workflow. She immediately picked Sam's CV out of the handful provided to her by HR. Experienced in the industry and with a decade of Chief of Staff experience behind her, Sam also had an Ivy League background, and to top it off, was bilingual in Japanese—a real asset at their transnational corporation. They started off strong and got a lot done in partnership over the course of the first month. But something was off. Kanae would want one deliverable; Sam would provide another—or none at all. Clearly, Sam was applying herself. She had a can-do attitude. But the situation was souring. And Kanae had no idea how to fix it.

KANAE *after* SAM

Kanae was frustrated, but she also knew it would be nearly impossible to find all of the qualities she required in someone new. She also suspected that part of the problem had to do with something she wasn't—or *was*—doing. So, Kanae brought in a coach: me. Kanae and Sam both participated enthusiastically because they both cared—about their work, the company's mission, and, ultimately, each other. And, with a heap of determination and a little bit of work on both their parts, Kanae and Sam made substantive changes. They initiated talks at the start and end of each day to establish and monitor tasks. They brought their most forward-thinking attitudes to the table and left judgment at the door. And as Sam's successful efforts began to take pressure off Kanae, the two discovered a kind of harmony emerging between them. A year later, hearing them crack each other up over the smallest thing, you'd be shocked to know there had ever been a problem.

Exercise

Meet with your Chief for one hour to discuss what's working and what isn't. If you are in a comfortable place with one another, do it monthly to keep your dynamic healthy. Do it more often if your relationship is struggling. Where things aren't working, discuss and implement adjustments as needed. Roll up your sleeves and talk things through. You'll get in the habit of it, and doing this regularly will keep the channels between you clean and clear. These prompts should help get you going.

1. How would you describe your current relationship with your Chief? Is it comfortable or struggling?

2. What are some specific areas that aren't working as effectively as you'd like in your relationship with your Chief?

3. What adjustments or improvements do you think could be made to enhance your relationship with your Chief?

4. How do you envision the ideal outcome of this meeting? What positive changes or resolutions would you like to see implemented as a result?

CHAPTER 9

My Objective for You

D o me a favor: Take a deep breath and settle in. This isn't a sales pitch for a vacation (though it might sound like it for the next few seconds). Instead, I want you to do a quick scan of your body. How are you feeling? Where's the tension? What's sore?

If you've just finished reading this book, then you probably know where this is going. But for those of you who skipped ahead to this chapter, hear me out. Many of the aches and pains you're feeling aren't just from poor posture or a lack of exercise. They're a direct result of being overloaded with work and responsibilities. You're trying to do everything for everyone, with no time to think about your own health or happiness, let alone your professional success.

But take a moment to imagine what life could be like if those stresses and pressures were lifted. Imagine your to-do list getting shorter, your frustrations easing, and your whole life transforming. Imagine what you could do with all that open time and liberated energy. And guess what? It's possible. All you need to do is to hire a Chief of Staff.

A Chief can be the key to unlocking a joyful life. I know it might sound a little fluffy, but I've seen it work countless times. Like a caddy on the PGA Tour, your Chief will be at your side, offering advice, empathy, and perspective while carrying your bag. They can create the space for your ideas to sizzle and for your energy banks to refill. Your team will reap the benefits of having a more engaged and less distracted leader. Your business will find its footing, fill in its gaps, and very likely flourish. It may sound like magic, and you know what? It is.

A Chief can be the key to unlocking a joyful life.

So put this book down and start your search. I promise you won't regret it. And who knows? Maybe we'll even cross paths along the way. Good luck and happy hunting!

Laurie Arron

Laurie Arron is the founder of Arron Coaching LLC, a premier executive coaching firm located in Dallas, Texas. She is recognized as a Top 20 Executive Coach in Dallas by *Influence Digest*.

Laurie spent 30+ years climbing the corporate ladder at an F10 company, where she gained multidimensional experience in sales leadership, strategic planning, and business transformation. Laurie also served as a Chief of Staff to senior executives.

Today, Laurie serves passionately as a trusted adviser and executive coach to C-suite executives and Chiefs of Staff. She helps her clients tap into their fullest expression as leaders, both for themselves and for the powerful impact they want to have on others. Laurie guides her clients to navigate the hard turns and pivot when they reach that internal dead-end of "no more." She helps leaders not only emerge but thrive.

Laurie earned her executive coaching certification from Coaches Training Institute (CTI), the largest coaches training school in the world (ICF accredited). She is a member of Litvin 4PC, an invitation-only, exclusive community for some of the world's most extraordinary coaches.

Laurie enjoys serving her community through boards and her philanthropic passions. She is also a dedicated member of the Texas Women's Leadership Institute. She enjoys traveling, cooking, working out, and spending quality time with her husband, her 16-year-old twins, and their Rhodesian Ridgeback, Zika.

Acknowledgments

As I reach the final pages of this book, I'd like to express my gratitude to those who supported me on this journey.

Writing this book would not have been possible without the support, encouragement, and assistance of numerous remarkable individuals to whom I am deeply indebted. I'd like to express my heartfelt thanks to each and every one of you who played a role in making this dream a reality.

To my family, friends, colleagues, mentors, and advisors, thank you for being a constant source of guidance, inspiration, and motivation. Your valuable insights, constructive feedback, and stimulating discussions enriched the content of this book and helped me shape my ideas more effectively. Especially Jeff Arron, Lawrence Godman, Lisa McCabe, Lani Kessler, Yousuf Khan, Mara Metzner, Dan Schwartz, Georgie Dickens, Misty Reich, Elaine and David Taylor-Klaus, Darrah Brustein, Kate Rosenow, Bettina Jahnke, and Rachel Simon.

A special thanks goes to the countless individuals who participated in interviews, provided testimonials, and shared their personal experiences. Your willingness to share your stories has added depth and authenticity to this book, and I am honored that you have entrusted me with your narratives. Extra thanks to Ralph De La Vega, Bill Hague, Jeff McElfresh, RC Buford, Alison Nabatoff, Dr. Marshall Goldsmith, Michael Yount, Thaddeus Arroyo, Rasesh Patel, Glenn Lurie, Rick Welday, Dr. Jamie Shapiro, Rich Litvin, Tino Mantella, Kelly Thengvall, Jeni Bell, Erin Scarborough, David Wasilewski, Sanyin Siang, Cliff Oxford, Janna Ducich, and Maryanne Cheung.

I'd also like to acknowledge the incredible team at Modern Wisdom Press, Catherine Gregory and Nathan Joblin, as well as Becky Robinson at Weaving Influence and Lawrence Bernstein and Anna Kennedy at Brand New Thinking, who all believed in this project from the beginning. Your contributions and support of me and my work have made this journey all the more rewarding.

Thank You

My heartfelt appreciation goes out to you, Dear Reader. Without your curiosity and interest, this book would not exist. I sincerely hope that the insights and knowledge shared here will be of value to you and that they spark new ideas and perspectives for you on your leadership journey.

If you're inspired and ready to amplify your leadership with the support of a Chief of Staff, please reach out and connect with me at the email address below. Let's elevate your leadership together!

In your corner,

Laurie Arron
laurie@lauriearron.com

Made in the USA
Columbia, SC
09 May 2024

35095492R00083